赵 钱 孙 李 周 吴 郑 王 冯 陈 褚 卫 蒋 沈 韩 杨
朱 秦 尤 许 何 吕 施 张 孔 曹 严 华 金 魏 陶 姜
戚 谢 邹 喻 柏 水 窦 章 云 苏 潘 葛 奚 范 彭 郎
鲁 韦 昌 马 苗 凤 花 方 俞 任 袁 柳 酆 鲍 史 唐
费 廉 岑 薛 雷 贺 倪 汤 滕 殷 罗 毕 郝 邬 安 常
乐 于 时 傅 皮 卞 齐 康 伍 余 元 卜 顾 孟 平 黄
和 穆 萧 尹 姚 邵 湛 汪 祁 毛 禹 狄 米 贝 明 臧
计 伏 成 戴 谈 宋 茅 庞 熊 纪 舒 屈 项 祝 董 梁
杜 阮 蓝 闵 席 季 麻 强 贾 路 娄 危 江 童 颜 郭
梅 盛 林 刁 钟 徐 邱 骆 高 夏 蔡 田 樊 胡 凌 霍
虞 万 支 柯 昝 管 卢 莫 经 房 裘 缪 干 解 应 宗
丁 宣 贲 邓 郁 单 杭 洪 包 诸 左 石 崔 吉 钮 龚
程 嵇 邢 滑 裴 陆 荣 翁 荀 羊 於 惠 甄 魏 家 封
芮 羿 储 靳 汲 邴 糜 松 井 段 富 巫 乌 焦 巴 弓
牧 隗 山 谷 车 侯 宓 蓬 全 郗 班 仰 秋 仲 伊 宫
宁 仇 栾 暴 甘 钭 厉 戎 祖 武 符 刘 景 詹 束 龙
叶 幸 司 韶 郜 黎 蓟 薄 印 宿 白 怀 蒲 邰 从 鄂
索 咸 籍 赖 卓 蔺 屠 蒙 池 乔 阴 郁 胥 能 苍 双
闻 莘 党 翟 谭 贡 劳 逄 姬 申 扶 堵 冉 宰 郦 雍
卻 璩 桑 桂 濮 牛 寿 通 边 扈 燕 冀 郏 浦 尚 农
温 别 庄 晏 柴 瞿 阎 充 慕 连 茹 习 宦 艾 鱼 容
向 古 易 慎 戈 廖 庾 终 暨 居 衡 步 都 耿 满 弘
匡 国 文 寇 广 禄 阙 东 欧 殳 沃 利 蔚 越 夔 隆
师 巩 厍 聂 晁 勾 敖 融 冷 訾 辛 阚 那 简 饶 空
曾 毋 沙 乜 养 鞠 须 丰 巢 关 蒯 相 查 后 荆 红
游 竺 权 逯 盖 益 桓 公 万 俟 司 马 上 官 欧 阳
夏 侯 诸 葛 闻 人 东 方 赫 连 皇 甫 尉 迟 公 羊
澹 台 公 冶 宗 政 濮 阳 淳 于 单 于 太 叔 申 屠
公 孙 仲 孙 轩 辕 令 狐 钟 离 宇 文 长 孙 慕 容
鲜 于 闾 丘 司 徒 司 空 亓 官 司 寇 仉 督 子 车
颛 孙 端 木 巫 马 公 西 漆 雕 乐 正 壤 驷 公 良
拓 跋 夹 谷 宰 父 谷 梁 晋 楚 闫 法 汝 鄢 涂 钦
段 干 百 里 东 郭 南 门 呼 延 归 海 羊 舌 微 生
岳 帅 缑 亢 况 后 有 琴 梁 丘 左 丘 东 门 西 门
商 牟 佘 佴 伯 赏 南 宫 墨 哈 谯 笪 年 爱 阳 佟
第 五 言 福 百 家 姓 终

CHINESE STORIES

Compiled by Jiao Bo
Translated by Zhou Xiaozheng

China Intercontinental Press

The Ordinary Chinese Today

Whenever I visited a foreign country as a Chinese writer, I always had a strong desire: apart from visiting those famous tourist attractions and contacting those famous and important personages, I wanted to go deep into the daily life in that country and have casual chats with the ordinary people of that country. This, I believed, would help me have a better understanding of that country.

Interestingly, almost every foreign friend I received in Beijing also expressed the same desire as mine. Therefore, I would accompany them to roam around in the streets and alleys of the city, sometimes dropping in a small restaurant for some typical Chinese food, sometimes purchasing a lovely souvenir from a roadside grocery stall. I always volunteered to be the interpreter for my foreign friends, to help them communicate with the ordinary Chinese on whatever topics they took an interest in.

As a matter of fact, anyone, no matter which country he or she is from, is somewhat curious about the living conditions of people elsewhere.

Fortunately, now we have this picture book. By reading it, I think, everyone can have his/her curiosity satisfied to some extent.

This picture book, compiled by Jiao Bo, has presented a host of different living conditions of the Chinese today in a natural way. To some extent, it should be regarded as a quite "unique picture book." Many picture books feature picturesque scenes and beautiful things, but this one features the people's lives; many picture books tend to display beauty and the artistic taste of the photographer, but this one pursues truth and tries to display the people's hearts and souls;

many picture books focus on social celebrities and beautiful women, but this one has focused on some very ordinary Chinese, on their life today, their experiences yesterday and their plans for tomorrow...

A Chinese idiom says that "one can learn what a leopard looks like by simply seeing a speckle on its skin," while a folk saying in the country goes that "one can know the change of all seasons by observing the change of a single leaf." Both mean that one can have some basic understanding of the entirety through the study of a part that has a general representation.

If we compare China to an ancient tree with a long history, then every Chinese, regardless of their sex, age, nationality, trade and experience, should be seen as the leaves on the tree. They are also the roots of this tree. The "reform and opening-up" drive has changed China, and as a result has brought about changes to the life and destiny of every single Chinese. Meanwhile, the changes of the ordinary Chinese have facilitated greater changes to take place in the country.

So is there also beauty in this picture book?

I believe there is.

Let's take Jiao Bo as an example. As a professional photographer, he has taken numerous pictures for his parents living in the countryside in the past 30 years and held a special photo exhibition which deeply touched many of the visitors. Jiao's conducts have prompted many others to ask themselves: as a child, what have I done to reward the great love of my parents?

Another example is that headmaster of that mountain-

By Liang Xiaosheng

top primary school, who overcame all difficulties to stay on just to teach four students. He has displayed the noble nature of education.

And those women who gave up marriage for life to mother the orphans in the "Children's Village" have brought maternal love to a new height.

Unlike what I have done above, the essays and captions in this picture book didn't depict the subjects in the photos in a highly emotional way. On the contrary, the book just recorded what kinds of people they were, what they did and why they did it by some plain words and simple narration. However, after reading these words and narration, I couldn't help getting moved and writing down passionate praises.

I wanted to pay homage to all self-dependent women in this picture book, such as the female shop boss on the Balkor Street of Lhasa, Tibet, or the female fruit grower who started her new career in the countryside after losing her job in the city...

I also wanted to express my heartfelt respect for the entire family of that old handicraftsman, who sold their woodprint New Year pictures worldwide, for the "child photographer" who entered the children's jury at a major international photo competition, for those brave young men who cleaned skyscrapers, and for those doctors and nurses who risked their lives to fight the deadly epidemic of SARS (severe acute respiratory syndrome). All of them are my lovely compatriots.

As a Chinese writer, I never locked myself in the study to write fictitious stories. Actually, I always have great concerns about China's reality and very much care about the fate of the ordinary Chinese. A large proportion of my works, which totaled more than 10 million characters, are about the life of the ordinary people. This has helped me establish an extremely intimate relationship, similar to that between kinsmen, with the ordinary Chinese. Therefore, I think I am in an appropriate position to evaluate this picture book.

In my view, this picture book really deserves the name of "Chinese Stories."

Besides ordinary people, this picture book also contains the stories of several successful personages with some fame, such as the famous dancer Chen Ailian, President of the Doublestar Shoes Manufacturing Group Wang Hai, and the real estate tycoon Wang Shi. However, these famous people are also quite familiar to us. In China today, successful entrepreneurs like Wang Hai and Wang Shi are mushrooming, and their success in career is of great significance to the further development of China's reform and opening-up endeavor.

At last, I want to give a simple conclusion: this picture book can be regarded as the "photo records" of the lives of many Chinese.

August 18, 2003, Beijing

目 录
Contents

Constructors of the Three Gorges Project

Washing of a foundation pit of the Three Gorges dam.
(photo by Huang Zhengping)

A full view of the Three Gorges dam construction site.
(photo by Yang Xiaodong)

On December 14, 1994, the Three Gorges Project, the world's largest hydropower project, was formally launched. With an order from the Chinese Premier, the first tank of concrete was poured into the No.8 foundation pit of the Three Gorges dam. Since that day, construction work has never stopped on the 15.28-square-kilometer construction site, and light has never gone out on the site at night.

It was a dream cherished by several generations of Chinese water conservancy and hydropower experts to build the Three Gorges dam on the Yangtze River, China's longest. Once completed, the project will not only generate power and enhance flood control, but also help improve the navigational conditions along the Yangtze and enable those relocated to make way for the gigantic dam to shake off poverty and lead a better-off life. All elite members of China's water conservancy and hydropower sectors have been mobilized to take part in this historic project, which is destined to add a glorious chapter to the Chinese history.

On the Three Gorges dam construction site, it is quite common to see fathers and sons, husbands and wives working shoulder to shoulder. Wu Huanxia, deputy head of a women's electric welding squad under the No.378 Cooperative Company, and her husband both work on the Three Gorges dam construction site. However, the couple were often assigned to different shifts, with one working in daytime and the other taking the night shift. But they have never complained. Wu's squad completed the welding work on more than 1,100 concrete units involving the power plant building and the five-level Three Gorges ship locks, and was thus honored as one of the "National Advanced Units of Female Workers."

"Quality first" is the motto for all constructors of the Three Gorges dam, and they have been extremely strict with themselves in every link of the project, such as checking the data, drawing the blueprints, the welding of every joint and even the fastening of every screw. Once the quality control personnel found in a random check that one screw bolt on the sluice gate failed to meet the intensity standard, and they immediately ordered the whole batch of some 10,000-strong screw bolts be thoroughly checked out. Wang Hui, an engineer in charge of monitoring the concrete pouring of the Three Gorges permanent ship locks, impressed everyone with his determination to defend the quality of the project. One day Wang found a quality problem with the just-poured concrete wall and demanded an immediate halt of the work. However, some workers, unwilling to see a delay of their work and a waste of materials, had tried to proceed with the concrete pouring. To their surprise, Wang risked his personal safety and jumped onto the truck, forcing the work to stop.

The constructors of the Three Gorges project also displayed a great team spirit. Some constructors said: "On the Three Gorges dam construction site, no work was done by a single unit, and every accomplishment was made through team work." In April, 2001, the Gezhouba Group, which was in charge of the building of the main body of the dam, suffered from a lack of heavy machinery for concrete pouring. Learning this news, the No. 378 Cooperative Company, which used to be a chief rival of the Gezhouba Group on the engineering market, immediately withdrew an imported concrete-pouring machine from its own work site and lent it to the Gezhouba Group. "We are both working on a great undertaking of our nation, and we must do everything to facilitate the progress of the whole project," said Yang Nan'an, general manager of the No. 378 Cooperative Company.

In June, 2003, the Three Gorges Project successfully completed its first-phase water storage, with the water level in the reservoir reaching 135 meters above sea level.

A simple lunch on the Three Gorges dam construction site.(photo by Yang Xiaodong)

Technicians checking the density of concrete with state-of-the-art devices. (photo by Sun Ronggang)

Constructors of the Three Gorges project braved rains to continue with their work.(photo by Yang Xiaodong)

⬆ Chinese and foreign experts involved in the Three Gorges project discuss technical problems together. (photo by Liu Shuguang)

⬆ At 10:54 p.m., June 24, 2003, the first electricity generated by the Three Gorges power plant was incorporated in the Central China Power Grid. (photo by Li Yonggang)

⬇ Two workers fixing power transfer equipment in the Three Gorges power plant. (photo by Du Huaju)

The "Shoemaking King" in China

As president of the Qingdao Doublestar Shoes Manufacturing Group, Wang Hai was the founder of a famous brand in China's shoemaking industry: the Qingdao Doublestar. The success of the Doublestar Group has turned Wang, who used to be a poor kid unable to afford a pair of shoes, into a world-famous "Chinese Shoemaking King".

In 1983, Wang was assigned to serve as the manager of the No. 9 Rubber Plant in Qingdao, a beautiful coastal city in east China's Shandong Province. At that time, the No.9 Rubber Plant, or today's Doublestar Shoes Manufacturing Group, was only a medium-sized State-owned enterprise specialized in manufacturing cheap rubber shoes. When Wang took office, there were some 2 million pairs of rubber shoes, all produced according to state plans under the then planned economic system, piling up in the workshops and warehouses and waiting for customers. As the enterprise faced imminent bankruptcy, Wang and his employees had

⚪ The Double Star Group invested to establish a factory in Yimeng Mountain area. Which was welcomed by the local people. And Wang Hai was happy, too.

⮕ Visiting a museum dedicated to the New Fourth Army, a Communist force winning lots of battles against the Japanese invaders in the 1930s and 40s. Wang might be thinking how to become an all-time winner in the market competition.

to carry these rubber shoes on their backs and went to the countryside to sell them to every village and town. It took a whole year for them to sell all these shoes out.

Wang had racked his brains to find a way to bring his enterprise, along with its 2,000 employees, out of economic troubles. He realized that shoemaking was a labor-intensive industry with meager profits. In the face of the invasion of famous foreign brands and escalating market competition, a domestic shoemaking enterprise must create its own famous brands for survival. Under his influence, the management of the No.9 Rubber Plant decided to shift the production of its old products, such as the outdated rubber shoes, to the township enterprises in the rural areas, while starting a totally new business in the workshops in Qingdao.

According to market demands, Wang and his employees started to make modern-style shoes first by imitation and later through technical renovation and upgrading. By the end of the 1980s, the newly emerged Doublestar Group had taken a leading position in China's shoemaking sector with the capability of manufacturing a series of modern shoes with advanced technologies, such as soccer shoes, basketball shoes, street-dance shoes and special exercise shoes for senior citizens. In 1992, "Doublestar" became the first "nationally famous trademark" in China's shoemaking industry as the group had acquired the ability to manufacture a variety of shoes, including cloth shoes, leather shoes, plastic shoes and professional sports shoes.

Doublestar's success also contributed to China's state-owned enterprises (SOEs) reform, as the group emerged as China's largest state-owned shoemaking enterprise with the best reputation and the highest economic returns. Many small and medium-sized SOEs have viewed Doublestar as their prototype in both management and marketing. For his personal contributions, Wang has won a series of honorary titles, including the National Model Worker, National Outstanding Entrepreneur and National Outstanding Manager.

Meanwhile, Doublestar shoes are also grabbing more and more market shares worldwide, with exports to more than 100 countries and regions including the United States, Japan, Germany, the Middle East, South America and Australia. The group has opened 9 overseas branches and offices in the United States, Hong Kong, Russia, Poland and other countries and regions.

Though already a successful businessman, Wang never changed his longtime habit of looking at the shoes of the passers-by while he was travelling around. It was his sincere wish that more people in the world would be travelling in Doublestar shoes.

⬆ Wang always wears a pair of Doublestar shoes.
While meeting some close friends, he will even take
off his shoes for a show-off.

⬆ Wang always regretted having spent little time
accompanying his late parents.

◀ There are a variety of shoe-shape souvenirs on
Wang's desk.

Even Wang's telephone set is in the shape of a delicate high-heel shoe.

Carrying out a quality check in the workshop.

Even while walking in the street, Wang likes to look at the shoes on others' feet.

Checking on the work in a Doublestar franchise store in
Yangzhou City, east China's Jiangsu Province.
Enjoying a happy family life with his son and grandchild.

The mother at the children's village

The Yantai SOS Children's Village was founded in 1986 with funds donated by an international non-government organization, the SOS Children's Villages International (SOS Kinderdorf International). In this small village surrounded and dotted by green grass and willows, there are 15 families, each with one unmarried woman nurturing eight orphans as their "mother". Zhang Yuxiao, one of the full-time "mothers" in the Children's Village, dedicated herself to this "special job" at the age of 33.

With a sweet voice and a talent for singing, Zhang had wished to become a performing star in her childhood. But her dream was never fulfilled. After her graduation from the high school, Zhang returned to her village and became a farming girl. The next year her father died of illness, and she became the main labor in the family, having to take care of both her sick, bedridden mother and her little brother who was still a school kid. In 1974, she became a saleswoman in the village store. In the next 10 years, she managed to have a tile-roofed, five-room new family house built, helped her brother find a wife, and even helped look after her brother's kids. However, as the first high school graduate in her village, Zhang was always a proud girl and never found someone she really loved and wanted to marry.

In 1985, Zhang became a teacher in the village kindergarten. Shortly after, an official with the county civil affairs bureau found her and told her that the newly-founded Yantai SOS Children's Village was recruiting "full-time mothers," who must be unmarried women without their own children. The official said that these "full-time mothers" could live in the retirees' apartments in the

Children's Village after their retirement. Zhang was immediately attracted by this offer: she was already more than 30 years old and still single, and was always a kids-lover. Maybe the Children's Village was just the best place for her. The next morning, she rode a bicycle to the county seat, some 60 km away from her village, and signed up as a candidate. For fears that someone would laugh at her once finding out her true identity, she didn't use her original name Zhang Weicui, but signed up with a new name Zhang Yuxiao.

After receiving some necessary training, Zhang returned home and hosted a feast for her family and fellow villagers. In her heart, she had viewed the feast as her wedding banquet, which she knew would never come along. In October, 1986, Zhang formally became one of the 15 full-time mothers at the Children's Village. As all kids in the village were orphans who had lost their parents, the duty of Zhang and other full-time mothers was to let them feel family warmth and maternal love once again. In the past 17 years, Zhang had mothered a total of 16 orphans and had devoted all her love and care to them. As her "youngest son" Bi Mingyang was of a weak physique since his birth, Zhang fed him personally at every meal and frequently brought him to medical experts for advice and assistance. When her "son" Wu Yunlong started learning to play electronic organ, Zhang accompanied him all the way to the Yantai City, some 20 km away from the Children's Village, for the lessons, and also helped him review the skills after return. When her "daughter" Yu Cuixia was about to take the college entrance exams, Zhang took upon herself all family chores, including cooking and clothes washing, to let Yu concentrate on her study. As a result, Yu smoothly passed the exams and entered the Yantai Education College.

For an ordinary mother, it is time for her to take some rest when her children all grow up. But for the mothers in the Children's Village, when their "children" grow up and leave them at the age of 18, they will immediately be assigned to mother a new group of little kids. As she was turning older herself year by year, Zhang was no longer as healthy as before. Sometime she also felt exhausted and upset, and even shed tears. But whenever she saw the lovely, tender faces of the kids and heard them call her "mother" in their sweet voices, she forgot all her hardship and unhappiness. She also took great comfort in the achievements of her grown-up children. Her "eldest son" Zhang Jiancheng, the first kid from the Children's Village to join the army, was honored as "a flood-fighting hero" for his outstanding bravery in the country's do-or-die battle against a devastating flooding along the Yangtze River in the summer of 1998. This news brought great joy and pride to Zhang, but also made her deeply worried about her son's safety.

◔ Zhang sent her children to the school in the rain.
◔ The kids are having a good time playing with their "mother".

23

◐ Zhang accompanied one of her daughters to practice piano.

◑ Every day Zhang helped her children in study.

◑ "The kids are growing and nutrition is very important to them," said Zhang.

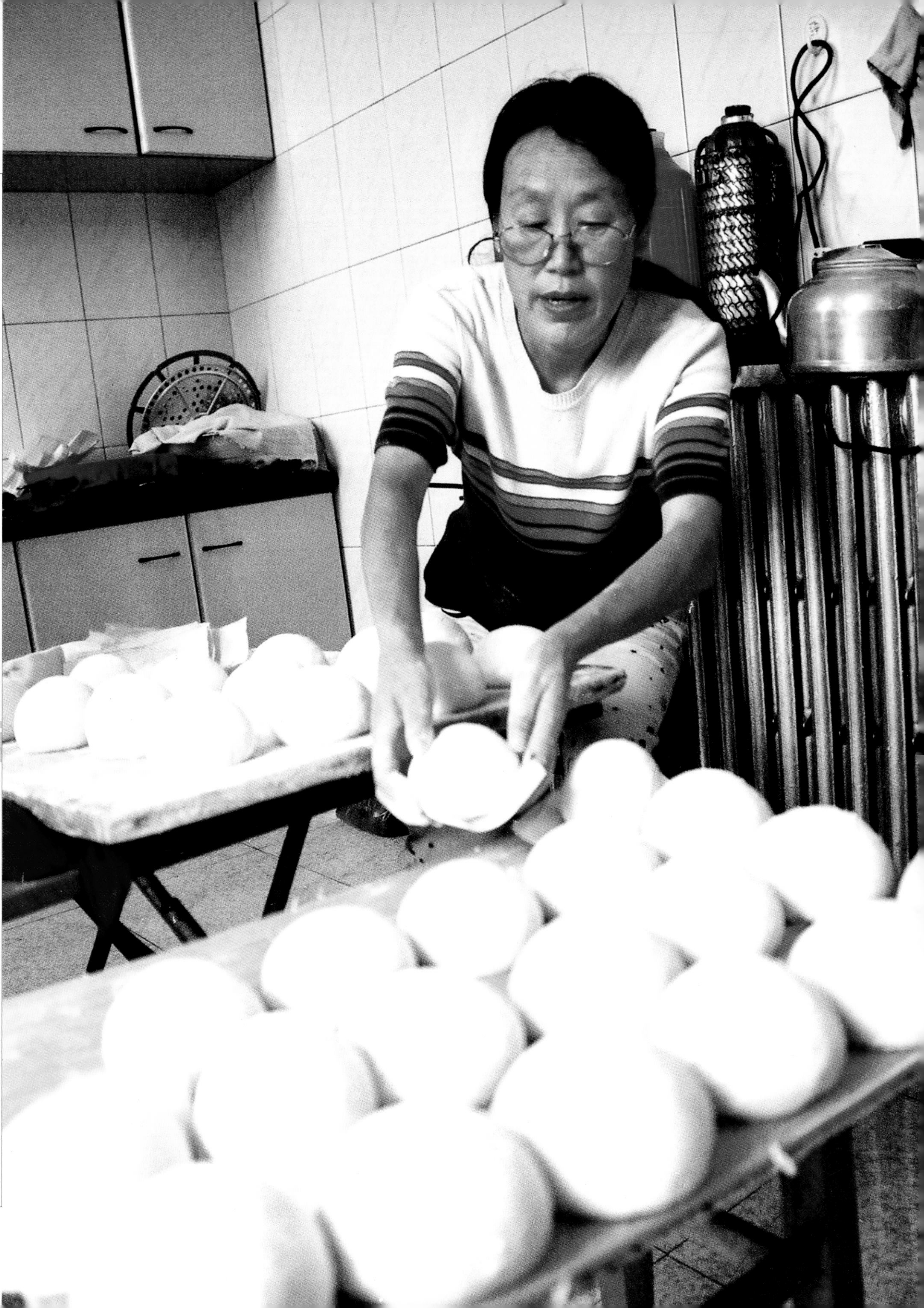

CHINESE STORIES

When the children all fell asleep at night, Zhang was still doing needlework.

"Mom, I have a stomachache."

Zhang spent most of the morning time preparing the lunch.

27

CHINESE STORIES

The "youngest son" tries to help mother do the washing.

Though the son is already taller than the mother, the mother is still concerned about his safety while crossing the road.

This is both a home and a paradise full of fun for the kids.

Gene scientists

Photos: courtesy of Beijing Huada Gene Research Center

Yang Huanming had studied and worked in Denmark, France, and the United States. In 1994, he returned to China and served as a professor of medical genetics and a tutor of Ph. D. Students at the Beijing Union Medical College. In the fall of 1997, Yang and several other scholars who returned from overseas study, including Yu Jun, Wang Jian and Liu Siqi, had a meeting as members of the Youth Committee of the Genetics Society of China. They discussed the development prospects of China's genome study and decided to work together to promote the progress of this promising undertaking. Their ambition was appreciated and supported by Lu Yongxiang, president of the Chinese Academy of Sciences.

In August, 1998, the Institute of Genetics under the Chinese Academy of Sciences established a "Human Genome Center" and Yang Huanming became the director of the center. By that time, the international "Human Genome Project," which involved scientists from the United States, Britain, Germany, Japan and France, had been under way for 8 years. This project was intended to identify all human genes and their locations on the chromosomes by analyzing the sequence of all 3 billion base pairs in the human genome. If successful, the project will provide the most important biological information about the human body and help mankind bring its self-study to the molecular level. Therefore, this project has been reputed as one of the "three most significant projects" in the history of mankind's natural sciences research, along with the Manhattan Project which led to the birth of atom bombs and the Apollo Program which sent man to the Moon.

Though just founded, the Human Genome Center of China

made a bold decision: to seek to represent China in the international "Human Genome Project" and share "1 percent" of the sequencing workload. In June, 1999, the Beijing-based Huada Gene Research Center formally submitted application to the human genome research institute under the U.S. State Health Research Center. In July of the same year, China was accepted as the sixth participating country in the international "Human Genome Project", also the only developing country in the project. In November, 1999, an appraisal panel jointly formed by China's Ministry of Science and Technology and the Chinese Academy of Sciences adopted a resolution to support China's participation in the international "Human Genome Project," and the "1 percent" sequencing formally became a State-sponsored program.

Yang Huanming was appointed as the chief coordinator on the Chinese side for the international "Human Genome Project." Under his guidance, the Huada Gene Research Center worked closely with the State Genome Centers in both north and south China to complete the sequencing work assigned to China in the spring of 2000. On June 26, 2000, 16 research centers in six member countries in the international "Human Genome Project" jointly announced the completion of the first ever draft framework of the human genome.

In the following developments, the Beijing Huada Gene Research Center co-worked with the Institute of Genetics under the Chinese Academy of Sciences and the State Hybrid Rice Research Center to paint a detailed genome map of indica rice, the first of its kind in the world. This achievement was selected as one of the "global top 10 scientific breakthroughs in 2002" by the U.S. Science Magazine. Yang Huanming and his fellow researcher Yu Jun were both crowned "outstanding research leaders" in the first ever selection of the "annual 50 leading scientific personages" by the Scientific American magazine. The Hong Kong-based "Seeking Truth" Foundation also granted a "collective award for outstanding scientific achievements" to Yang and his research team for their superb performance between 2001 and 2002.

Yuan Longping, an academician with the Chinese Academy of Sciences reputed as "father of hybrid rice" in China, paid a visit to the Beijing Huada Gene Research Center.

Yu Jun, deputy director of the Beijing Huada Gene Research Center, in his lab.

Yang Huanming in front of a gene sequencing device.

32

A group picture of chief researchers from all 16 centers in 6 countries involved in the international human genome project. (first row, second from right: chief coordinator on the Chinese side Yang Huanming)

A colorful spare-time life for the researchers - a tug-of-war game in the park.

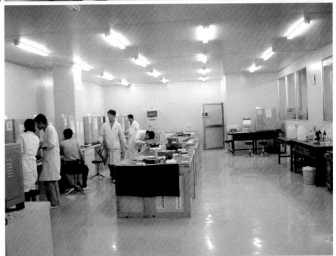

① An industrialized sequencing base.
② Researchers on the Chinese side for the international Human Genome Project, which was formally launched in China in 1999.
③ The main research center on the Chinese side for the international human genome project.

A famous Peking Opera performer

Photos by Cheng Tieliang

Zheng Ziru is a Lao Dan performer, or a performer specialized in playing the part of an old woman, in the traditional Peking Opera. In the 1980s, she was the leading actress in a newly-adapted historical drama "A duel with short spears," in which she played the role of Jiang Guihua, an ancient heroine who was deserted by her husband for 40 years and finally avenged herself by beating that treacherous man in a short-spear duel. The drama turned out to be an instant success after its premiere in the Chang'an Grand Theater in Beijing. Zheng was invited to tour around the country as the drama was repeatedly staged for more than 200 times, making Zheng the most famous young performer in China's Peking Opera circle at that time. In 1988, Zheng staged her first personal special performance in Beijing. In 1990, she won the Wenhua Award, the country's top award for culture and performing arts granted by the Ministry of Culture.

Though Zheng had quickly reached the peak of her career as a Peking Opera performer, she never felt self-contented and never ceased seeking new breakthroughs for the traditional art of Peking Opera. In cooperation with students from some arts colleges, Zheng directed a modern drama "The uncle's dream," which had no division of acts and applied avant-garde accompaniments and stage designs. Zheng herself played the heroine of the drama, Madame Maria. "This performance gave me new experience totally different from that of Peking Opera performance," recalled Zheng.

In 1993, at the invitation of the French Baroque Modern Dances Troupe, Zheng went to France to play in a modern dance drama "The meteors". It was also in France that she married a French diplomat whom she had met and fallen in love with in Beijing. After the marriage they had a lovely and beautiful daughter. Though on a foreign land, Zheng had never forgot the Peking Opera. She often explained the art of Peking Opera for wives of foreign diplomats, and even taught them some basic singing and performing skills of Peking Opera. Thanks to her persistent efforts, many foreign friends of hers started to have some basic understanding of Peking Opera, some even becoming Peking Opera fans.

In 1998, Zheng and her family returned to China, with her husband serving as the cultural attaché in the French Embassy in China. The first thing Zheng did was to resume her career as a Peking Opera performer. "After living overseas for so many years, I still regard Peking Opera as the most important part of my life," she said. On the 20th anniversary of the premiere of "A duel with short spears," Zheng cooperated with the China Peking Opera Theater to present this famous drama once again. Fan Yongliang, Zheng's old partner in the drama who played the role of the deceptive husband, also flew to Beijing from Shanghai to join her. The drama succeeded again and won wide acclamation from both the audience and the art critics. In early 2002, Zheng engaged herself in another ambitious plan—to adapt the story of French Saint Joan of Arc into a Peking Opera play.

⊕ Zheng's daughter was very excited to see a poster featuring her mother in a personal special performance.
⊖ Zheng Ziru on stage.

⬆ "Behind one minute of successful performance on stage is 10 years of hard training." Zheng's excellent skills have come from her hard training every day.

⬆ "Mom looks so pretty."

➡ Zheng is always the idol of her daughter.

⬆ Zheng will never forget the early years of her performing career.

⬇ In real life, Zheng seems to be practicing and performing Peking Opera anywhere, anytime.

The teenage photo competition judge

The World Press Photo competition hosted by the Netherlands annually is one of the most prestigious international photo competitions. The competition also grants a special Children's Award to a picture taken by a child photographer. Each year, 9 children from all over the world are invited to the Netherlands to form an International Children's Jury. They will choose from the 400-strong candidate photos, which cover a wide range of themes including major news events, nature and environment and sports, one picture to be crowned the "best children's photo of the year." In the 2002 competition, the chairman of the International Children's Jury was a Chinese student named Li Xiaonan.

Li, 12, was a Grade-six student in the Huayuan Road No.3 Primary School in Jinan City, capital of east China's coastal province of Shandong. He was chosen as the Chinese representative in the jury and later elected the jury chairman for his superb understanding of the photographic art and his excellent capability of self-expression. Before he went to the Netherlands as a jury member, Li already won several awards in major photo competitions at home. A group of photos he took, titled "Traffic Policewomen in the City of Springs (which refers to Jinan)", won a bronze medal at the "Chinese Little Journalists" photo competition. Another piece of his works, My Primary School Life, won the first prize for the primary school level contestants in China's National Teenagers' Photo Competition. In June, 2001, Li held a personal photo exhibition in Jinan, which consists of two parts, namely The Unforgettable School Life and The World In a Kid's Eyes.

Li has started his photographic career under the influence of his father Li Nan, a photographer with the Jinan-based Dazhong Daily. Li Nan was also the first Chinese to have his name marked on the golden trophy of the World Press Photo competition in the Netherlands. However, the junior Li has displayed his photographic talents at an early age. When he was only a Grade Two student in the primary school, one day Li went along with his father to take some pictures of the female traffic police on the local streets. When the father had his son's first photos developed, he couldn't believe his own eyes: some of the pictures were really impressive. So he sent them to a teenagers photo competition in the province, at which they won a second prize.

Seeing his son greatly encouraged by the initial success, the father put an automatic exposure camera in his schoolbag and told him to take pictures of every interesting thing or moment on campus. After years of practice, the junior Li has produced quite a few excellent works.

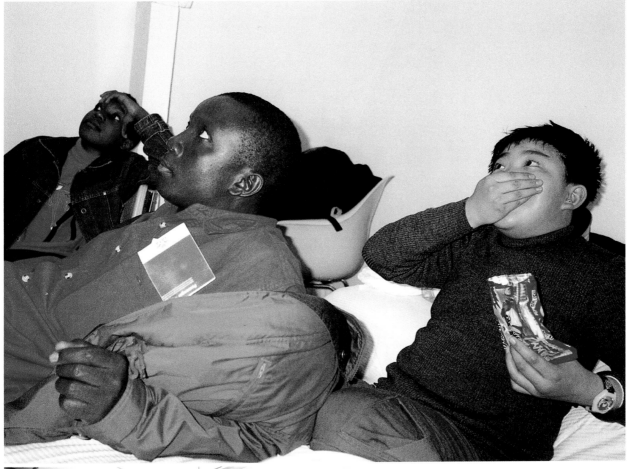

41

CHINESE STORIES

- "Spare-time activities": one of Li's works.
- Only a Grade Six student in the primary school, Li already held his first personal photo exhibition.
- Li has a special interest in folk handicrafts.

◑ A happy family.
◐ Li is a good student with excellent test
   results for all subjects at school.

44

⊕ Li Xiaonan interviewing a traffic policewoman in Jinan.
⊘ Sports are another hobby of Li Xiaonan.

⬆ Li in a group photo with other members of the International Children's Jury at the 45th World Press Photo competition.

The conquerors of Mt. Qomolangma

○ Photos by Zhou Xingkang & others

The snow-capped Mount Qomolangma is named after a legendary Tibetan goddess. As the world's highest peak, it has attracted numerous mountaineers longing to conquer it. While mankind is marking the 50th anniversary of its first successful ascending of Mt. Qomolangma, a team of Chinese mountaineers, led by Deputy Secretary-general of the China Mountaineering Association Wang Yongfeng, surmounted the mountain again on May 21 and 22, 2003.

There were four amateur mountain climbers in the team. Among them Liang Qun is a teacher of the Shenzhen University in south China's Guangdong Province. Liang and her husband Li Weiwen started mountaineering in 2000 and their common love for adventure led them into matrimony. Pitifully, when the team was on its final leg to the mountain peak, Li was left behind for his poor physical conditions and couldn't stand side by side with his wife on the top of the world. Chen Junchi is a staff member of the Hainan Provincial Branch of China Unicom (China United Telecom). When the mountaineers reached the peak of Mt. Qomolangma, he sent a multi-media short message, along with a color photo of the team standing on the peak, via his mobile phone to inform everyone about their success. Wang Shi, 52, is the chairman of the board of the Shenzhen Vanke Co. Ltd. in Guangdong. At the 8848.13-meter-high mountain peak, Wang suggested his teammate Liu Jian propose to his girlfriend on the phone, and volunteered to be their witness. Deeply touched by this proposal from the world's highest point, Liu's girlfriend responded with no hesitation: "Yes, I will."

It was on May 25, 1960 that the Chinese first climbed onto the top of Mt. Qomolangma. On that day, three members of the Chinese National Mountaineering Team, namely Goinbo (Tibetan), Wang Fuzhou and Qu Yinhua, overcame all difficulties to unfurl a Five-Star Red Flag, China's national flag, on top of Mt. Qomolangma. They were also the first men to ascend the peak from the north side. Since then, the Chinese mountaineers have conquered Mt. Qomolangma for 14 times, with 61 people setting foot on its peak.

⬆ Mt. Qomolangma. (photo by Zhou Xingkang)
⬆ Mountaineers replacing their climbing equipment. (photo by Zhou Xingkang)
➥ Mountaineers on their way to the northern slope of Mt. Qomolangma. (at an altitude of 6,730 meters) (photo by Zhou Xingkang)

The couple of Li Weiwen and Liang Qun prepare to advance to the next camp at an altitude of 7,028 meters. (photo by Zhou Xingkang)

All supplies first reach the logistics base and then are carried to the ABC camps on Yak back. (photo by Zhou Xingkang)

The camp in the snow. (photo by Zhou Xingkang)

51

CHINESE STORIES

A triumphant return to Chengdu, capital of southwest
China's Sichuan Province. (photo by Tan Xi)
Surmounting the peak successfully. (courtesy of the
Chinese National Mountaineering Team)

My dad and my mom

Photos by Jiao Bo

52

In 1931, in a mountain village of east China's Shandong Province, Jiao Wenchong, 17, married the 19-year-old Qiao Huagui. Both Jiao's father and grandfather were carpenters, and Jiao, after receiving a brief education of four years, dropped out of the school at the age of 11 to learn carpentry at home. The hardship of life had turned him into a strong and able young man. On his wedding day, Jiao wore an imported straw hat, which he borrowed from someone else, a fashionable long robe and a pair of dark cloth shoes, and, according to local customs, stood at the gate of his home waiting for the arrival of the bridal sedan chair. Qiao Huagui, a traditional girl with bound feet, arrived at Jiao's home with a red cloth covering her face. She was wearing a flower-dotted cotton coat, which she borrowed from someone else, and a pair of embroidered shoes that she made herself.

Though Jiao's parents had given birth to 11 children, Jiao turned out to be the only survivor. Indulged by his parents since his childhood, Jiao had an extremely bad temper and was easy to turn violent. Once he slapped Qiao in the face. Feeling greatly humiliated, Qiao swallowed a bottle of kerosene in an attempt to commit suicide, but fortunately she was saved in time. Despite all the quarrels and fights with her husband, Qiao never thought of a divorce. "Even if you are married to a chicken or a dog, you must spend the rest of your life with them. This is the fate of women," said Qiao.

After living together for a long time, the two gradually got used to each other's style. Whenever Jiao turned angry and shouted at her, Qiao simply ignored him and wouldn't mind his words or attitude. Sometimes she would even say: "The old guy always speaks loudly, as if he is having a quarrel with someone. But when he speaks in a low voice, it means he must have been sick. Therefore, I would rather always hear him talk loudly."

After having four children, the old couple no longer quarreled in their children's face. In their children's eyes, they had always been a loving couple leading a harmonious life. Even after they went to bed at night, the children could still hear them talk to each other in low voices, as if they had an endless need for communications.

An ancient Chinese saying goes that "when you get old, your best company is your spouse." It was true. When they both grew old, Jiao and Qiao couldn't stand even the shortest separation, as if they were each other's shadow. They helped each other in everything and slept together every night. As all their children now work and live in the cities, the old couple were often invited to live there for some time. However, every time they must go together and return together, otherwise they would miss each other very much and even couldn't sleep well. In the Chinese countryside, it is a tradition for the senior citizens to prepare coffins for themselves in advance. As a veteran carpenter, Jiao had reserved the best coffin he had ever made for his wife, something that had made Qiao feel very contented. She told everyone that "I never regret spending my lifetime loving my carpenter husband."

Jiao Bo, one of the old couple's sons, works as a photographer with a Beijing-based newspaper. Over the past two decades, Jiao Bo had taken more than 8,000 pictures of his parents and published a photo album titled "My dad and my mom." In 2001, to mark the 70th wedding anniversary of the old couple, their son held a photo exhibition for them in the village and also invited them to fly to Beijing for a sightseeing tour. On their flight to Beijing, Jiao held his wife's hands tightly and murmured only one word: "I want to always hold your hands like this."

- In the fall of 1996, mom and dad visited Beijing for the first time. They joined a group of toy-playing kids on the Tian'anmen Square.
- In 1999, when mom fell ill and had a fever, dad kissed her on the forehead, claiming that he was testing her body temperature.

In 1978, after 47 years of marriage, mom and dad had their first picture together.

"Upward, still more upward!" dad always asked mom to help him scratch his itching back.

① Mom and dad making brooms for sale.
① Mom helping neighbors make pastries.
④ In 1983, the rural household contracting system was introduced in my home village. Mom and dad busied themselves day and night in the field.

The village where mom and dad lived has a history of 600 years. Though in recent years many villagers built new houses outside the village, mom and dad were unwilling to leave their ancestral home.

Mom and dad slept together in the same quilt all their life.

When telephone was just installed at home, mom made the first try, but held the handset upside down. Her great-grandson burst into laughter.

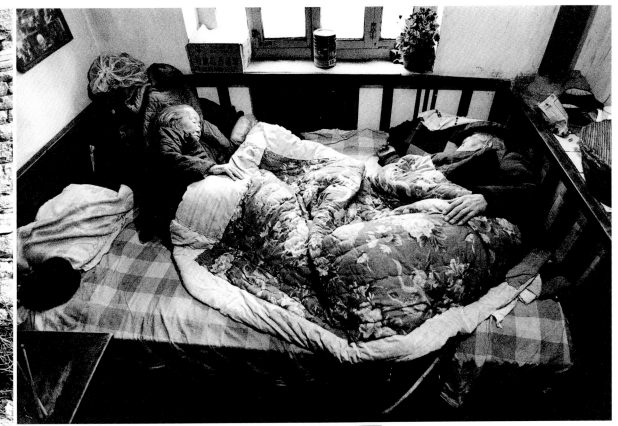

60

⊕ In 1996, mom and dad visited the Tian'anmen Square.
⊖ In November, 2002, the 90-year-old mom and the 88-year-
  old dad had their last picture together taken. One month
  later, dad passed away.

The real estate tycoon who aims high

Photos: courtesy of Shenzhen Vanke Co. Ltd.

Wang Shi is a famous figure in China's real estate sector. In December 1998, Wang was selected by the China Central Television as one of the "20 most influential people" in China's two-decade-long reform and opening-up process. In May, 2003, when the Chinese Mountaineering Team successfully surmounted the world's highest peak, the Mt. Qomolangma, Wang was one of the amateur members in the team.

In his life, Wang has always aimed high and cherished great ambition. He started his climbing of the ladder of success at the age of 32, when he left his home province, the Guangxi Zhuang Autonomous Region, for Shenzhen, a booming special economic zone in south China's Guangdong Province.

In Shenzhen, after one year of hard work, Wang founded an "exhibition and sales center for modern scientific and educational devices" to sell Japanese electric appliances such as the products of Sony and Panasonic. In 1988, he introduced a shareholding reform in his company and renamed it the Shenzhen Vanke Co. Ltd. In the same year, his company expanded its business to the real estate sector. In 1991, Shenzhen Vanke was formally listed on the Shenzhen Stock Exchange and gradually became a well-known name among Chinese investors.

The Shenzhen Vanke company has achieved remarkable success in the real estate sector. With four years of experience in selling Japanese products, Wang has learnt modern management concepts from the Japanese enterprises, especially the philosophy of "clients first" and the brand name awareness. In order to turn Vanke into a well-known brand name, Wang said, it is equally important to promote the sales of houses and to provide first-class after-sale service for the clients in a consistent manner. Since 1993, Vanke has further expanded its business to other parts of China and quickly established itself as a leading real estate developer across the country. In 2002, Vanke was selected as one of the "300 most successful small enterprises worldwide" by the U.S.-based Forbes magazine.

Wang also attracted much public attention for his unique lifestyle. He loves travel and photography, and has visited many foreign countries all alone. He also loves adventures, claiming that challenging sports activities, such as mountaineering and parachute gliding, could help him maintain enthusiasm for his business career and constantly encourage him to explore "unknown domains."

Wang once said: "With the success of Vanke, I myself also became a so-called social celebrity. However, deep in my heart I really miss my life in the 1980s, when I just started my business ventures. I will never change my attitude toward life and my old habits." The next goal of adventure for Wang is seafaring. "To fulfill this dream, I must keep on working hard and earn more money," he claimed.

- Wang accompanied Li Changchun, a senior leader of the Communist Party of China, in an inspection tour of the "All-Season Flower City" housing project.
- At a meeting with other real estate tycoons.
- Wang Shi looks full of ambition at an exhibition on real estate development.
- Wang always looks calm and broad-minded.
- One of Vanke's real estate development projects—the Shenzhen "Home, Sweet Home" housing project.

Wang (left) on top of the world.

A fan of photography, Wang often goes to the countryside to take pictures.

Wang likes to take adventures or exercise challenging sports in his spare time.

The "Printers' Family"

Photos by Qian Jin & Qian Yi

In Nanchang, capital of east China's Jiangxi Province, there is an old man reputed as "Mr. Old Printer," who, along with 10 other members of his family of four generations, has dedicated the whole life to the printing business for more than half a century. His name is Qian Chuntao.

While he was just around 10 years old, Qian Jizu, father of the "Mr. Old Printer", entered a private printing house in China's largest city Shanghai as an apprentice. What he learnt in the plant was typecasting, or the making of Chinese-character movable types used for printing. When he completed his apprenticeship, Qian became a formal employee of the printing house. In 1949, the printing house affiliated to the Nanchang-based Jiangxi Daily newspaper purchased an electric typecasting machine from Shanghai, but could find no locals capable of operating this new device. So the newspaper decided to recruit a technician from Shanghai, while Qian Jizu turned out to be the one.

After working in Jiangxi for half a year, the senior Qian summoned his son, Qian Chuntao, to the province and started to teach him typecasting skills. At that time the working conditions in the printing house were terrible, with no ventilation or tap water supply. The printers even had to carry water from outside the workshop to cool down the typecasting machine.

Qian Chuntao became a printer at the age of 16. His father, a very stringent person, had required him to work hard and be the best of all printers. Under his father's guidance, the junior Qian had studied really hard to grasp skills and worked with an earnest attitude, and had repeatedly won honorary titles like the model worker of the printing house, of the city and even of the province.

It was in the typecasting workshop that Qian Chuntao fell in love with his colleague Li Gengmei and eventually married her. They had three sons. In 1977, the eldest son Qian Jin was recruited by the printing house as a worker in the photo plate-making workshop. In 1980, the second son Qian Kang, after retiring from the army, also entered the printing house. In 1981, the youngest son Qian Ming replaced his retired mother to join his brothers as a printer. The three juniors had become the third generation of printers in the Qian family. After staying for 13 years in the printing house, Qian Jin, the eldest son and an amateur photographer who won several provincial and national prizes in photo competitions, was transferred to the "culture and entertainment" department of the Jiangxi Daily at the end of 1990. Shortly after, Qian Ming, the youngest son, also shifted to the editor-in-chief's office of the newspaper.

In 2002, Qian Xi, the granddaughter of Qian Chuntao, also became a staff member of the Jiangxi Daily printing house after her graduation from a vocational training high school. She was the fourth-generation printer in the Qian family, but she would have a printing career totally different from that of her predecessors, thanks to the new age of laser photo composition.

A group picture of the "Printers' Family".

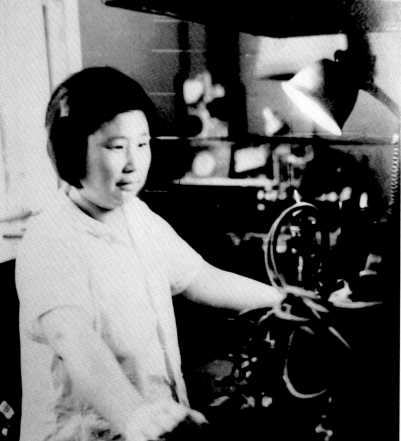 

① Li Gengmei, wife of Qian Chuntao, at work in the
workshop when she was young.
② Qian Chuntao's eldest son Qian Jin at work in the
photo plate-making workshop, in 1980.

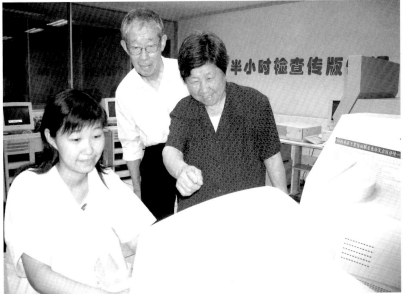

⊕ "Mr. Old Printer" at work when he was young.
⊕ The old couple were stunned by the advanced laser photo composition technology when they visited their granddaughter's workshop.

The old couple have lived happily together for more than 50 years.

Due to the hard work in the early years, the "Mr. Old Printer" suffers from a sore waist. His wife often gives him a massage session.

Medical workers in SARS wards

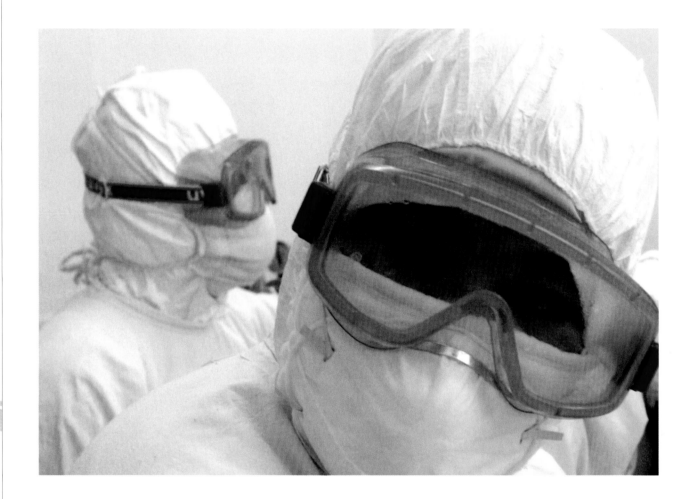

Every doctor in the SARS wards was completely clad in infection-prevention clothes and equipment.
The inpatient department building of the Ditan Hospital.

On the evening of April 17, 2003, Jiang Rongmeng, a doctor of the Ditan Hospital in Beijing, and his wife Wen Wei, also a staff member of the same hospital, dined out to celebrate their 6th wedding anniversary. Unlike what had happened on all the previous anniversaries, however, the couple didn't exchange presents or greet each other with words of love. After a simple dinner, they immediately returned home and went to bed early. This was because Dr. Jiang, after working for more than 20 days in a row in his hospital's special wards for SARS (severe acute respiratory syndrome) patients, had been completely exhausted, while his wife would soon join him in the fight against SARS. On the very day of April 17, the Ditan Hospital was designated by the Beijing Municipal Health Bureau as one of the local hospitals exclusively accepting and treating SARS patients.

Founded in the early 1950s, the Ditan Hospital ranks among the best hospitals for epidemic treatment in Beijing and even across the country. In the spring of 2003, the Chinese capital encountered a sudden outbreak of SARS, a deadly epidemic which emerged at the end of 2002 and claimed several hundred lives worldwide during its peak spreading period between March and June, 2003. The Ditan Hospital received its first probable SARS patient on March 26. As the disease was spreading around the city at an unexpectedly rapid speed, the Municipal Health Bureau issued an urgent order on April 17 to turn six local hospitals, including the Ditan Hospital, into special hospitals exclusively for SARS treatment.

Upon receiving the order, the Ditan Hospital mobilized all doctors and nurses available, including those from the outpatient department, the health care department and the ultrasonic examination division, to work in the inpatient department and serve in the SARS wards. Other hospitals also sent in reinforcements.

Starting from the evening of April 21, when the first group of SARS patients transferred from other hospitals arrived and checked in, the Ditan Hospital had established 9 "isolation zones" to accept the incoming SARS patients, with each zone fully occupied within 24 hours after its establishment. In the life-and-death battle against SARS by China and the rest of the world, the Ditan Hospital was just like a fearless spearhead defying all dangers and difficulties.

Yang Fan, head nurse of the hospital's surgical department, led all her team to serve in the 4th isolation zone. Since the first day she entered the SARS wards, her son had been sending her the same short message by mobile phone every day: "Mom, take good care of yourself. I'm waiting for your safe return home." To ease the worries of her family, Yang responded every time that she was fine. However, the situation was very grave. As a veteran nurse with 22 years of working experience in an infectious disease hospital, Yang had never seen a fellow nurse get infected while tending on the patients. However, in the early days of the fight against SARS, she saw five colleagues contract this disease and fall ill. Fortunately, thanks to timely and effective treatment, all of them had recovered in the end.

Though the entire Ditan Hospital was put under quarantine during the SARS outbreak, the doctors and nurses there were not feeling lonely. Actually, they had felt the care and support from all walks of life. When the Nurses' Day arrived, the hospital received over 5,000 paper cranes, a traditional oriental symbol for happiness and good luck, and more than 1,000 letters of compliments from the local citizens, as well as 100 boxes of fresh peach from fruit-growing farmers in the suburban counties. During the SARS outbreak, many medical workers in the Ditan Hospital had a better understanding of the old Chinese saying that "true affections show only at times of crisis".

In Beijing's anti-SARS campaign, the Ditan Hospital took in and treated a total of 300-strong SARS patients. While recalling those unforgettable days and nights, a doctor in the hospital said: "I can't say I'm a noble person. But I am a person with the basic professional ethics. At that time, there was no difference between a doctor and a soldier. When you are needed in the front, you must go there and fight. Otherwise you become a deserter."

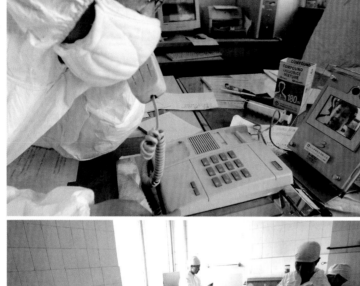

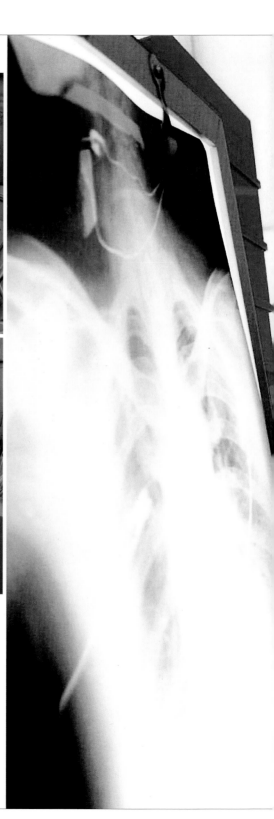

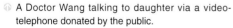 A Doctor Wang talking to daughter via a video-telephone donated by the public.

Medical workers dining in the SARS-fighting front.

On May 8, Li Xingwang, an expert on infectious diseases in the Ditan Hospital, was examining an X-ray of a SARS patient carefully. As a chief doctor in the front, Li only slept for 9 hours in three days.

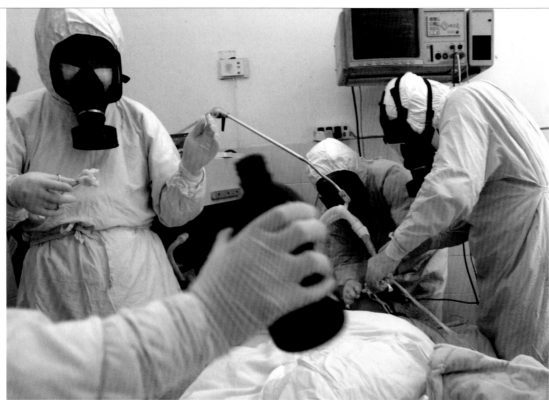

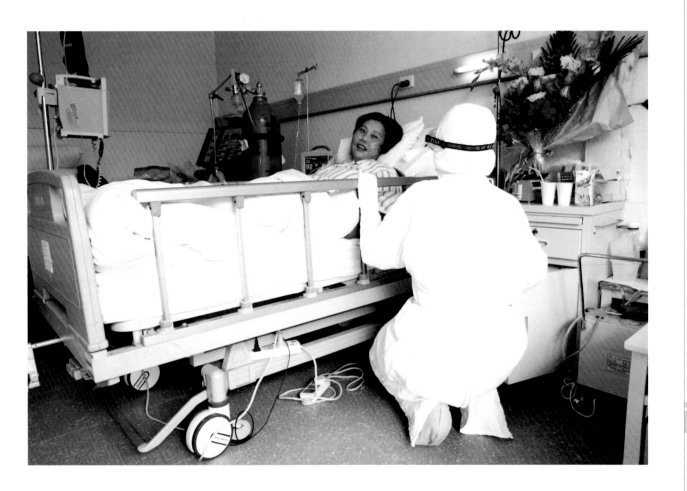

77

CHINESE STORIES

⬆ Medical workers listening to a SARS patient at a close range.
◗ On April 30, several doctors risked possible infection to perform a tracheotomy operation, or cutting open windpipe to facilitate respiration, on a critical SARS patient.
◖ Late at night on May 12, a nurse was reporting the situation in the SARS wards to doctors-on-duty via a walkie-talkie.

A five-person hilltop school

Photos by Jiang Hao

There is a primary school in Yupan Village, situated on top of a 640-meter-high hill. The school has only five members, including four pupils and one teacher. Every morning, Zhang Guangxiang, the teacher, will travel 6 kilometers on foot from his home village of Shaozhuang to the school to give lessons. With his arrival, the school turns alive as the students start reading their texts.

The Yupan Village is under the administration of Zhangxia Town, Changqing County of Jinan City, capital of east China's Shandong Province. As the village is too remote and secluded, many teachers were unwilling to teach at the village primary school, which only had a few students. In the fall of 1988, two months after the schools in other villages had opened, the Yupan village primary school still couldn't find a teacher. Learning this news, Zhang Guangxiang, then a faculty member and also the accountant of another school in the county, volunteered to go to the Yupan village school.

At first Zhang's wife firmly opposed his decision. With two elderly members and a little kid to be taken care of and several mu (several thousand square meters) of orchard to be attended to, she said, the family couldn't make do with Zhang's absence. However, Zhang repeatedly told his wife that "it was not easy for kids in the mountains to get an education opportunity". "I, who used to be a kid in the mountains myself, couldn't stay idle and watch those kids become illiterates." Finally, his wife was persuaded and agreed to let him go.

When Zhang just arrived, the schoolhouses at the Yupan primary school were simply several stone cabins with thatch roofs, through which one can see the blue sky. The ground in the "classrooms" was not level, while the desks and stools were scattered everywhere. Zhang first cleaned the houses and repaired the desks and stools, and then visited every households in the village to find back the only four children of school age. Once again readings and laughter of the kids could be heard from the stone cabins.

At the primary school, Zhang is both the headmaster and the teacher, and he treats every student as kindly as their fathers. The four kids belong to three different grades, and Zhang has to prepare lessons at three different levels. While some of the students couldn't afford the tuition fees or textbooks, Zhang would pay for them with his own meager wages. When the mother of Yu Xuewei, a grade-two student, suddenly deserted her family and went missing, Yu was called back by her father to help him do farmwork and look after her 9-month-old brother. To help Yu return to school, Zhang sent milk powders and biscuits to her home and even shared her workload by helping her take care of her brother. Jiang Lianli was a crippled student with congenitally deformed legs. Whenever the students needed to go down the hill to the county central school for major exams or public activities, Zhang would carry Jiang on his back all the way. "She also has the right to see the outside world," said Zhang.

With a hammer and a chisel he brought from his home, Zhang often leveled the ground in the school compound or collected rocks to build compound walls when he was free. The villagers, touched by his dedication to the village school, all came to his assistance. It didn't take long before the walls were built around the school compound and fruits trees, flowers and grass were planted to beautify the school. Every Monday, Zhang and his students will hoist the Five-Star Red Flag, China's national flag, in the school compound while singing the national anthem loudly together. The singing will echo in the mountains for a long time. Since his arrival at the Yupan Primary School, Zhang has taught a total of 60 graduates. In 2001, he was granted a "May 1" badge for model workers by the All-China Federation of Trade Unions.

A group photo of all members in the school.
The Five-Star Red Flag was raised in the five-person-only primary school.

79

CHINESE STORIES

In this classroom, Zhang Guangxiang has taught and seen off his students one group after another. He has dedicated his youth to this hilltop primary school.

Though there are only four students in the school, Zhang always teaches with an earnest attitude.

82

⊕ Walking on the mountain path with a student on his back—something Zhang did frequestly.
⊖ After the class, the teacher and students play together.

"The flying girl"

Photos by Wu Huang

Ye Yi is the youngest aerialist, or better known as the "flyers", in the acrobatic troupe under the Zhejiang Folk Art General Performing Troupe of east China's Zhejiang Province. Six years ago, while the acrobatic troupe was recruiting new blood, Ye, then 15, was picked at the first sight by the troupe's flyer trainers and was thus ushered into a performing career full of freshness, excitement and hardship.

A repertoire of Ye's acrobatic troupe, the flyers' performance is highly risky as no safety guarantee measures would be taken during formal performances and any slight mistakes could lead to fatal consequences. Just as an old saying goes: "Behind one minute of successful performance onstage is 10 years of hard training", every movement of the flyers in their performance must be practiced for hundreds and even thousands of times beforehand.

Every morning at 6 o'clock, Ye Yi would be awakened punctually by her alarm clock. Though Ye is the youngest "flying girl" in the troupe, but compared with those little trainees who have just entered the troupe, she is already a "Sister Ye". As the monitress of the trainees' class, every morning Ye is always the first to go to the training hall, where she will lead other boys and girls in regular training and exercises, such as the warm-up exercise, leg pulling and ligament stretching. The training was tough, strict and painful, while the would-be flyers often shed sweat, tears and even blood. Ye Yi is always kind to those younger trainees, who often remind her of her early days in the troupe, and is willing to share her experience with them.

Every girl has a dream, and Ye Yi is no exception. However, Ye is not a person with unrealistic ambitions. She only hopes that she could learn to speak good English and someday go abroad to spread the Chinese acrobatic culture. Sometimes she also thinks that she might become an excellent acrobatic trainer when she gets old. Anyway, this "flying girl" is steadily advancing toward her goal of life, step by step.

85

A perfectionist, Ye Yi will continuously practice the same movement until she feels satisfied herself.
"The flyers" is a traditional performance in Chinese acrobatics.

⬆ Ye Yi firmly believes that she is capable of anything that a boy can do.

⬆ Combing hair in front of the large mirror in the training hall before the morning exercise. There is no make-up time in the morning as the training starts early.

⬇ The training is hard, but life is happy.

⬇ The trainers, who are extremely strict with the performers in training sessions, are the true heroes behind the scenes.

Signal watchers at the foot of the Goddess Peak

The Qingshidong Signal Station lies at the foot of the Goddess Peak, a famous mountain by the Wuxia Gorge of the Three Gorges section of the Yangtze River, China's longest. There are four signal watchers in the station: the Station Chief Wang Liquan, 37, and three young men, namely Xiao Liang, Xiao Cai and Xiao Zeng.

The Qingshidong Signal Station, which is under the jurisdiction of the Fengjie Navigation Control Division under the Chongqing Navigation Management Department, is in charge of safety control for all ships passing the Wuxia Gorge watercourse. The station decides the passing sequence of all ships that sail through the Wuxia Gorge, and directs their movement with the red or white signals it hangs out. "Normally the passing sequence is decided according to the time of arrival of the ships. But in high water season, ships going upstream should give way to those going downstream," said Wang.

Founded in 1950, the signal station has a lot of antique equipment which has been in service for more than half a century. For example, the telephone set is a hand-reeled one, while the binoculars are also a product of the 1950s. As the outdated diesel generator broke down two years ago, Wang and his colleagues had to light self-made "kerosene lamps", or wine bottles filled with kerosene, in the evening. There is no water source near the station, and the station staff have to carry water from the Yangtze river with buckets every day.

Though life is hard for the signal watchers, they have always been earnest in performing their duties. They record every ship traveling through the gorge watercourse. On windy days, it is impossible to hang out the signals and the station has to use its high-frequency telephone to guide the passing ships. Therefore, the station staff have never left the high-frequency telephone in an unattended status.

The signal watchers work on three shifts a day and take turns to go home for a rare family reunion. Every month Wang could only meet his daughter for a few times and as a result the girl has always felt strange to her father. "Water is as precious as oil here"commented Wang's wife, after a visit to the station. Wang added that for a signal watcher, it was really difficult to find a wife. Among the three young men in the station, only Xiao Liang has a girlfriend, who works as a highway maintainer, a job as harsh and underpaid as signal watching. Wang said that for some time he himself also thought of leaving the station for a job change. But realizing that his station oversees a highly risky watercourse and requires the service of experienced signal watchers, he finally decided to stay on. "The signal watchers are just like the eyes of the ships. Without these eyes, the safety of the ships couldn't be guaranteed," said Wang.

While Wang and his staff are leading a dull and lonesome life with even no TV or newspaper, numerous ships and boats, many carrying tourists coming to enjoy the beauty of the Three Gorges and the Goddess Peak, have passed the Wuxia Gorge safely. While the tourists are watching the Goddess Peak through their binoculars or camera lenses with great interest, they won't know what that small, inconspicuous signal station at the foot of the mountain means to their safety.

With his sharp eyes, Wang Liquan has a close watch at every ship passing by.

Though the station has only four staff members, it holds a solemn national flag raising ceremony every day.

Wang Liquan cleans the signals every day.

 Wang is the best chef in the station.

⊕ Wang and his staff plant corns and pumpkins around the signal station for some fresh vegetables on the dinner table.

⊜ "The signal is small, but it has a bearing on the safety of tens of thousands of ships traveling on the Yangtze," said Wang.

The inner-painting artist in Xi'an

The inner painting is the art of painting scenery or characters on the inner sides of hollow, transparent handicrafts, such as snuff bottles and crystal balls, with a special curving pen that is extremely slim. As a snuff bottle's mouth is as small as a bean and its internal diameter is no longer than an inch, inner-painting is a highly demanding job. And to make sure the users could enjoy the beauty of paintings inside the bottles, the inner painting artists must have an excellent command of the skills of "reverse painting". Normally it takes one month or so to paint a snuff bottle. Seven or eight years ago, there were still quite a few local inner-painting artists in Xi'an, capital of northwest China's Shaanxi Province, but today it is already very difficult to find one.

Li Junyu, 24, is a native of Hengshui City, north China's Hebei Province. He started to learn inner painting at the age of 14, with a next-door lady being his first tutor. His inner painting skills belong to the Hebei School, which ranks among China's three leading "inner painting schools" along with the Beijing School and the Shandong School. Inner painting artists of the Hebei style are good at copying from ancient Chinese paintings, especially human portraits. After grasping excellent inner-painting skills, Li had moved to Xi'an, an ancient capital which attracts many domestic and foreign tourists, along with his family.

In Xi'an, Li has been making a living by painting and selling inner-painting handicrafts. In the past few years, he has created many wonderful inner-painting works, with the copied ancient Chinese painting "A picture of the riverside marketplace on Ching Ming Festival" being his own favorite. The painting, a masterpiece in the Chinese painting history, depicts the city life in China during the Northern Song Dynasty (around 10th century A.D.), featuring a total of 550 characters. Li successfully reproduced this long scroll of painting inside a small snuff bottle, and every tourist seeing it couldn't help marveling at his superb skills.

Li and his wife have rent a small apartment near Xiaoyan Pagoda, one of the local scenic spots in Xi'an. The apartment is both their home and painting studio. While his wife runs some small business in the city, Li stays at home all day and concentrates on inner painting. Under his influence, his wife also started to learn inner painting and has now been able to paint some small crystal balls. Li said that he liked the ancient architecture in Xi'an very much, and planned to paint four leading ancient architecture in the city, namely the Bell Tower, Drum Tower, Dayan Pagoda and Xiaoyan Pagoda, in one bottle. "I will use the art of inner painting to reflect the splendid history and ancient civilization of Xi'an," he claimed.

Most inner paintings on snuff bottles originate from Chinese folk tales and legends.

CHINESE STORIES

The rented apartment is both home and studio for the Li couple.

Inner painting is much more difficult than external painting, and the artist must be extremely careful with every stroke.

Though still very young, Li has been deeply influenced by the splendid ancient culture of China.

Li Junyu has painted the Xiaoyan Pagoda not far away from his home in a crystal ball.

To prevent recurrence of tragedy

Wang Xuan is a Chinese who studied in Japan and found a job there after graduation. In August, 1995, she read a story on a Japanese newspaper about the First Germ Warfare Symposium held in Heilongjiang Province, northeast China. At that symposium, three representatives from Yiwu City, east China's Zhejiang Province, had demanded compensations from the Japanese government for the sufferings inflicted on their hometown by the Japanese army through the germ warfare during World War II. This news shocked Wang, who is also a native of Yiwu.

In 1942, 396 people in Chongshan Village of Yiwu, including eight members of the Wang family, died in the plague outbreak caused by the Japanese army's germ warfare. While killed by the plague, Wang's uncle, or her father's younger brother, was only 13 years old.

Wang decided to join the lawsuit launched by the Yiwu people to seek justice for their murdered ancestors. She believed that with her knowledge of the Japanese language and laws, she could be of great help to her countrymen. "More importantly, I am also a native of Yiwu and it's my unshirkable responsibility to help my countrymen win this lawsuit," she added. So she gave up her tranquil life and immersed herself in the lawsuit. Along with her Japanese friends, she traveled to most parts of China to collect evidence for the germ warfare of the Japanese army. During her investigation, Wang learnt many miserable stories about innocent people getting killed by the Japanese-spread plague germs. "Japan was the only warring party in the Second World War that used biological, chemical and germ weapons," Wang said. During the Japanese invasion against China, all parts of the country, except Xinjiang, Tibet and Qinghai, were subject to the attack of the germ warfare by the Japanese army. Even today, the Zhejiang Province still needs to catch 1,000 sample mice a year for blood test and plague prevention. In 1996, the Epidemics Prevention Manual published in the province still had the category of "bubonic plague", as some of the sample mice still tested positive for plague infection. However, for more than half a century after WWII, the Japanese government has never openly confessed to having conducted germ warfare in China.

Having collected detailed information about 180 Chinese victims in the Japanese germ warfare, Wang launched a lawsuit against the Japanese government, on accusations of spreading fatal germs like those of bubonic plague on the Chinese soil during WWII. After a marathon trial that lasted for 5 years, in August, 2002, the chief justice of the Tokyo District Court ruled that the Japanese army, such as the No.731 Unit, had used biological and chemical weapons in China according to instructions from the Japanese army command. However, the court had turned down all compensation demands. Wang immediately appealed to the Tokyo High Court, continuing to demand an apology and compensations from the Japanese government.

"We will continue our lawsuit until justice is done. But what's more important is to let the public learn the historical truth, so as to prevent the tragedy of germ warfare from happening again", said Wang. She said that the world should know those Chinese who fell victim to the germ warfare and died in pains and humiliation. "Tens of thousands of Chinese victims had died in silence, some even unrecorded in history. Our lawsuit is intended to give out a voice on their behalf, a voice of dignity and indignation. Now this voice is loud enough to be heard all over the world," Wang added.

⮑ Wang holding pictures of late Chinese plaintiffs, who were witnesses to the Japanese germ warfare but passed away in the process of the marathon trial, at the entrance of the Tokyo District Court to protest the unjust first instance ruling.

Wang introducing the case to a noted American lawyer.

Wang delivering an emotional speech at an international conference.

It was already late at night, and Wang was still studying international and Japanese laws in her hotel room.

Despite her loss in the first trial, Wang was warmly
received at her hometown.

On the eve of the Chinese lunar New Year, Wang
was on her way to Yiwu City, Zhejiang Province for
investigation and evidence collection.

The doctor of medicine

○ Photos by Li Ming

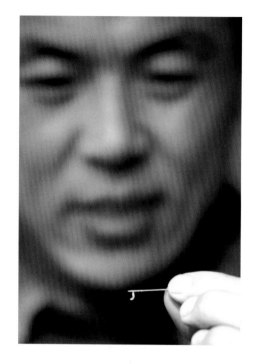

⬆ The "enemy" for Zhang to deal with is even smaller than a grain of rice.
◐ Zhang Ying staying in a mosquito net and observing the drug-resistance capabilities of locusts and cabbage worms against "Nature No. 1".

In 1992, Zhang Ying was bestowed with the doctorate of biophysics by the Salzburg University of Austria. The same year he was invited to be a research fellow with the European Aeronautic and Space Center and participated in the space bioengineering program of Europe. Meanwhile, he also served concurrently as the superintendent of the medicine development department under the Carlson International Co., taking charge of the research on the compound formulae of traditional Chinese herbal medicines.

In early 2001, the provincial government of Yunnan in southwest China invited some Chinese students studying overseas to return to their motherland and participate in the construction of a "China Medicine Valley" in the province. Zhang was one of the overseas students who accepted the invitation. While working in Yunnan, he asked for a leave to go back to his hometown Xuzhou, a major industrial city in east China's coastal province of Jiangsu, to visit his parents.

Shortly after Zhang went back home, he was contacted by some local officials, who told him that farmers in Xuzhou, a major growing base of Chinese chives, had been haunted by chive-eating maggots for years. The officials sincerely asked Zhang to stay in Xuzhou and help to develop some effective biological pesticide against the chive-eating maggots. After careful considerations, Zhang agreed to stay and serve as the technological supervisor in the Xuzhou Biotech Engineering Co. Ltd., specialized in the development of biological maggot killers.

Zhang decided to develop a new pesticide from herbs and plants. He studied several hundred kinds of Chinese medicinal herbs and natural plants, carried out numerous experiments and tests, and used modern bioengineering technologies to make his invention effective in pest killing but harmless to human beings or beneficial insects. It only took a bit more than half a year for Zhang to successfully develop a plant-origin pesticide with completely independent intellectual property right, which he named "Nature No. 1".

To acquire firsthand information about the effectiveness of this new pesticide, Zhang and his assistant had leased a small piece of farmland to grow Chinese chives themselves. Field experiments showed that all technological indexes of "Nature No. 1" had met international standards. Currently, this invention has been recognized by China's Ministry of Agriculture and will soon be promoted as one of the officially sanctioned pesticides. Many investors from all over China, including Hong Kong, have now signed contracts with the Xuzhou Bio-tech Engineering Co. Ltd. regarding the joint production of biological pesticides and feeds.

① Zhang Ying never returned from his experimental field empty-handed.

② With a chicken farm of his own, Zhang Ying can carry out his experiments very conveniently.

③ Even during the Spring Festival holidays, or the Chinese lunar New Year, Zhang remained in his lab and worked hard.

"The Spider Men"

photos by Chen Gengsheng & Wu Fang

In China today, skyscrapers are mushrooming in the increasingly modernized cities, and their external walls need regular cleaning. The workers engaged in the cleaning of high-rises have to hang themselves in mid air with only a safety rope on their waists, and clean the glass walls with brushes. Marveling at their courage and skills, the people often call them the "spider men".

Shen Erhui, 21, is one of the "spider men", and he works for the Henan Huangjin Cleaning Co. Ltd. Every morning, Shen and his colleagues will tie the safety rope to their waists, sit on a suspended board and hang themselves down from the top of a high building. For several hours to come, they will concentrate on washing and brushing the external wall of the building, with no time for drinking or even going to toilet. On his job Shen could earn a bit more than 1,000 yuan (120 dollars) a month, which is a comparatively high amount for a local migrant worker. However, his job is quite risky and only suitable for young men with a bold mind, strong body and quick reaction. There are also some basic skills for building cleaning, said Shen. "For example, you should fold your dirt cloth eight times beforehand to use it more efficiently while cleaning the glass. And you should always stick your feet to the surface of the external wall and make every movement very slowly, only with the strength of your ankles," he explained.

Scientific study has found that the life duration of a high-rise could be 20 percent longer if the building gets regular cleaning. With the expanding urbanization across China, the need for high-rises cleaners is also on the rise. Some young men eager to find a job have joined this team. Zhang Chunwei, 28, used to work as an analyst in a chemical plant, but after the bankruptcy of his plant, he became a high-rises cleaner. Though there was much difference between his previous and current jobs, Zhang said he had no problem adapting himself to the changes. Su Xinyuan, 22, was from a needy family which could not afford his schooling. However, this young building cleaner firmly believed that "if you are smart and diligent, you will succeed in any place". He cherished an ambitious dream—to become an expert on cleaning some day.

When dusk falls on the city, the "spider men" also land onto the ground. In the evening, they relax themselves either by playing bowling and roller skating or singing and playing cards. An excellent roller skater, Shen Erhui can attract many girls who want to learn skating skills from him.

The safety rope is several hundred meters long and weighs over 50 kg. It is no easy to handle.

What seems to be risky performance to others is just daily routine for the high-rise cleaners.

⬆ Going home—the most pleasant moment in the day for a high-rise cleaner.

⬆ Before starting to work, the high-rise cleaners will spend some 20 minutes checking their safety helmet and safety rope. "Safety first!" they say.

➡ A group of high-rise cleaners hang themselves in mid air like spiders.

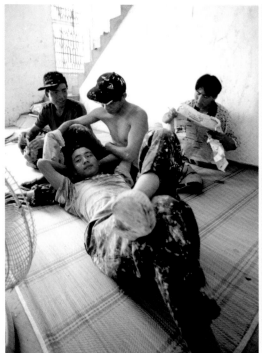

The noon break.

Shen Erhui, a high-rise cleaner, is also an expert on roller skating.

The cleaned glass wall of the high building looks like a giant mirror.

The on-train mail escorts

Photos by Jiang Hao

⬆ All mail escorts must work with quick hands.

Cao Wenhe is an on-train mail escort travelling along the railway linking Jinan and Harbin, capitals of east China's Shandong Province and northeast China's Heilongjiang Province. Cao's work is simple - to unload mails that have reached their destination and load outgoing mails whenever the train stops at a railway station. There is no air-conditioning system in the train's mail compartment, which is always freezing in winter and sweltering in summer. When the train leaves the station, the mail escorts will have nothing to do but wait for the next stop.

The Jinan Municipal Mail Escort Department, which Cao works for, has a total of 120 mail escorts who are assigned to serve in the mail compartments of more than 20 trains. Cao and three of his colleagues work on the train travelling between Jinan and Harbin, and the journey usually takes nearly 30 hours. When the train enters a new station, three of the mail escorts will start unloading the arriving mails, while the rest one will count the mails and take records. As the train normally only stays for minutes at each station, the mail escorts must be swift and quick-handed. After doing the mail unloading job for decades, Cao's hands have developed many calluses and look somewhat distorted.

Once aboard a train, the mail escorts often have to be absent from home for several days in a row. Due to their irregular lives, many of them suffer from stomach troubles. Zhao Huamin, a team leader on the trains travelling between Jinan and Shanghai, is a veteran mail escort with 25 years of working experience, and has been suffering from stomach troubles for 23 years. Every time when he is assigned to escort a train, his wife has to prepare stomachache medicines for him in advance. Li Lihua, who has been working as a mail escort for 18 years since his graduation from the school, has in all traveled 2.7 million kilometers by train, which equals touring around the globe for more than 60 times.

A popular saying goes that "a good girl shouldn't marry the on-train mail escorts, who often leave their wives uncared-for at home". However, all of the wives of the mail escorts have given an all-out support to their husbands in their work. For 24 consecutive years, the wife of Xue Taisong, a veteran mail escort, has kept

on sending meals to her husband on the train whenever the train passes the Jinan station. She also accompanied her husband on the mail train on the eves of 12 Spring Festivals, or traditional Chinese lunar new years.

China's modern post service was initiated in 1896. In the past century and more, the vehicles used for mail transport have evolved form donkey or horse carts to wheelbarrows and trucks and finally to trains and planes today, and the speed for mail delivery has become faster and faster. In recent years, China has launched several nationwide railway speed-ups in which the speed of all trains has improved sharply. This also leads to greater workload and higher pressure on the mail escorts. During his work breaks, Cao Wenhe likes to take some brief sleeps at home. But even during these sleeps, he will often wake up suddenly and ask which station the train has arrived at.

113

They have been busy for several days, It is time to have a rest at home.

The wife has kept on sending meals to her husband on the mail trains for 24 years.

Mail escorts sharing home-prepared meals.

It's late at night, but the mail escorts are still sorting out the post bags on the narrow aisle of the mail compartment.

Ruan Xihai, a university graduate, is still very fond of reading even as a mail escort.

Wang Deli, 21, starts blowing a mouth organ while the train is traveling. All veteran mail escorts know that this young man is homesick again.

Zhang Ming and his music library

Photos by Ge Xin

Zhang Ming is an enthusiastic fan of music, and his love for music has been extended to audio equipment. In order to achieve the most satisfactory sound effects while listening to music, he has not only taken pains to choose the best stereo, but also designed a wave-shape suspended ceiling for the living room at his home.

Zhang is an associate professor in the music department of the Zhejiang Academy of Arts in east China's Zhejiang Province, and he mainly teaches western music history and foreign music classics. He is especially fond of the western classics, with the Piano Trio of Mozart and the String Quartet of Beethoven being his top favorites. He is easy to be intoxicated by both the harmony and happiness in the music of Mozart and the sad beauty of Beethoven's melodies.

Zhang says that music has changed his life, made his beliefs simple, and taught him how to enjoy the fun and happiness of life. He likes most what Mozart once said: "Music! What do I need other than music?!" In his decade-long music teaching career, Zhang has managed to collect more than 5,000 CDs (compact discs) of Chinese and foreign music classics, as well as over 2,000 books on music. With such a rich personal collection, Zhang had always thought of establishing a private music library to cater to the need of other music fans. So he wrote a letter to the mayor of Hangzhou, capital of Zhejiang where Zhang lives, and asked for permission to run such a library.

It didn't take long for his application to get the green light from the local government, and the first private music library in China came into being in Hangzhou. Zhang moved all his collections out of his home and placed them in the library. "From now on, all music lovers can come here to share my personal treasures," said Zhang.

Zhang turned very talkative at the mention of any masters of music.

To pick out a specific CD (compact disc) wanted by some library visitor from his 5,000-piece strong collection was no easy job even for Zhang himself.

120

Zhang often received foreign friends and shared his music expertise with them.

Music fans visiting Zhang's library for the first time were often surprised at the large collection of CDs he had.

A romantic birthday party Zhang arranged for a music-loving girl.

For Zhang Ming, sorting out the collections he just moved from home to the library was also a pleasant experience.

Tea growers on the Xuefeng Mountain

On the 1,000-meter-high Xuefeng Mountain of Minhou County, east China's Fujian Province, there was a deserted tea garden. In 1993, a couple arrived from Taiwan and signed a 50-year-long contract with the county government to revitalize this tea garden.

Fujian is the place of origin and also a leading producer of the oolong dark tea, a Chinese specialty. Lin Shengguang, a businessman from Taiwan who loves nature, had always wished to come to the Chinese mainland and invest in a tea garden on the mountains. He chose the Xuefeng Mountain as his investment destination.

To guarantee the quality of the oolong dark tea, the tea trees must have a good origin and must be planted in a clean, unpolluted environment. The harvest of tea leaves as well as the ensuing processing also must be done by highly skillful workers.

The Lin couple carefully selected and purchased fine species of tea trees from southern Fujian and also from Taiwan, while they also insisted no fertilizer or pesticide be used in tea growing. They also bought advanced tea-making equipment from Taiwan and hired highly competent technicians for tea processing.

To date, the couple have lived on the Xuefeng Mountain for 10 years. In the past 10 years, they have spent almost every day in the tea garden. During the tea harvest season, they put on the same shabby clothes as the local tea-growing farmers and worked in the tea-making workshops day and night. Tea processing involves more than 10 procedures, and the couple always see to every procedure personally for quality control. Currently, the Xuefeng Mountain Tea Garden produces 80,000 kilograms of tea annually, which is sold to Beijing, Shanghai, Shandong, Fuzhou and Xiamen, as well as exported to Japan, the Republic of Korea, Sweden and other countries. Several tea varieties produced at the garden have won golden prizes at the China (Beijing) Tea Culture International Seminar and have been acknowledged as "green food", or pollution-free food, by the China Green Food Development Center. In early 2003, the Xuefeng Mountain tea also passed the European Union's agricultural products check, and was expected to enter the European market soon.

Today the Xuefeng Mountain Tea Garden has an overall investment of 38 million RMB yuan (4.58 million dollars) and has planted a total of 3,500 mu (233 hectares) of tea trees. The tea garden also established 38 franchise stores for tea sales across the country. "My tea garden aims at contributing to the improvement of the overall quality of the Chinese tea," claims Lin Shengguang.

The harvest season is the busiest time at the tea garden.

⊕ During the tea harvest season, the tea garden holds tea quality competitions every day.

⊕ There are both hardship and fun in the couple's life on the mountain. They often play chess as spare-time amusement.

⊘ Madame Lin is a good chef and often cooks for workers in the tea garden.

⊘ Madame Lin, who majored in business administration in her college study, insists on working together with the tea garden workers, to make friends with them and raise efficiency.

⊘ The Lin couple selecting newly-picked tea leaves.

⊘ After 10 years of hard efforts, the tea garden now has 3,500 mu (233 hectares) of thriving tea trees.

A dutiful son from Taiwan

◎ Photos by Zhong Min

On September 17, 2002, Liu Xiashi celebrated her centennial birthday at her home in the countryside of Sichuan Province, southwest China. Her elder son, Liu Zhiguo, had flown all the way back home from Taiwan for this occasion.

A native of Suining City, Sichuan Province, Liu Xiashi now lives in the Jichang Village of Nanqiang Town, Shizhong District. She has two sons. The elder son Liu Zhiguo joined the Kuomintang army in 1945 and was dispatched to Taiwan in 1948. The next year, the People's Republic of China was founded and the links between the Chinese mainland and Taiwan were severed. Liu Zhiguo had also lost his contact with his mother. In the following decades, Liu Xiashi had lived with the family of her younger son, but she had never stopped missing her elder son on the other side of the Taiwan Strait.

After being discharged from the army, Liu Zhiguo had first worked on a farm and later started his own business. In the late 1970s, the Chinese government launched its reform and opening-up drive, and contacts between compatriots across the Taiwan Strait gradually resumed. In 1988, Liu Zhiguo went back to his home province of Sichuan and fulfilled a family reunion with his mother and brother, after four decades of parting. After that, Liu returned to hometown every year to visit his mother, and every time he tried to stay longer to perform his duty as a son.

In 2001, Liu Zhiguo successfully persuaded his mother to go to Taiwan with him and spend the rest of her life there. However, after staying in Taiwan for a short period, the old lady found it difficult to get used to the life there and started missing her hometown. As she insisted, Liu had to send her back to live with his younger brother. But he promised his mother that he would return home once again in September 2002 to celebrate her 100th birthday.

Learning the news of Liu Xiashi's centennial birthday, the local officials and fellow villagers also sent in flower arrangements and other gifts to express their best wishes. Liu Zhiguo also had 538 China bowls made, each carrying the Chinese character "Shou", or "longevity". He also invited the Suining City Singing and Dancing Troupe to perform at the birthday party. The party attracted almost all residents in the neighboring villages, who packed the small compound of the Liu family to the full. There were so many guests attending the birthday banquet at noon that it took nearly 100 tables to have them all seated.

Ⓐ Liu Zhiguo had 538 "longevity bowls" made to mark his mother's 100th birthday.
Ⓐ Liu Zhiguo invited a singing and dancing troupe to perform at his mother's birthday party.
Ⓐ Liu Zhiguo kissing his mother at the birthday party.

128

⬆ The family of Liu Xiashi has tens of members of six generations living together.

⬆ The centennial lady tells others how kindly her son treats her.

➲ "It's the fine tradition of the Chinese nation to take good care of the elderly, and we must carry forward this tradition," says Liu Zhiguo.

The maker of woodprint New Year pictures

When he was still a child, Zhang Tingxu had learnt from his father how to make woodprint New Year pictures. Today, making New Year pictures has become the main income source for Zhang and his wife.

Zhang's family workshop is located in the Zhaozhuang Village near Zhuxianzhen town of central China's Henan Province. There are many age-old Chinese New Year pictures, which dated back to the Ming and Qing dynasties (1368-1911) and were produced or collected by his ancestors, at Zhang's home. These ancient pictures, along with the new works printed by Zhang himself, have attracted many visitors including foreign tourists and domestic folk arts lovers. "The New Year pictures I printed were sold to private collectors in more than 20 countries across the world, as well as put on display in countries like France and Japan," said Zhang with a pride. "I really love this trade."

Zhuxianzhen is well-known in China as a leading producer of the woodprint New Year pictures, with this form of folk art originating in the town more than 1,000 years ago. The basic techniques for New Year pictures printing in Zhuxianzhen consist of manual carving of patterns and characters on the wooden board and color printing with water and ink. The color inks used for the color printing are extracted from traditional Chinese medicinal herbs, and as a result all the printed pictures have extremely bright colors that could last for a long time without fading.

While the trade of woodprint New Year pictures printing reached its peak during the Ming and Qing period, there were a total of more than 300 printing workshops with several thousand craftsmen in Zhuxianzhen, producing over 1 million pieces of New Year pictures each year. Their products were sold all over the country and even exported to foreign countries. However, in the past century, due to the impact of the popularization of modern printing technologies, the market demand for the traditional woodprint New Year pictures shrank rapidly, forcing many old workshops to close. Currently there are only fewer than 10 New Year pictures printers in Zhuxianzhen.

To prevent this traditional folk art from extinction, local folk art lovers have formed a Zhuxianzhen Woodprint New Year Pictures Research Society, with Yao Jingtang as its president. Yao has searched many historical records to collect a series of stories which used to be the main themes of the New Year pictures produced in Zhuxianzhen. He plans to publish a 40-story album of the Zhuxianzhen New Year pictures. He picked Zhang Tingxu as the album printer, and once he collected a story he handed it over to Zhang, who, with assistance of his wife and daughter, adapted the story into a series of New Year pictures. When the first volume of the album, which comprises 26 stories, was finally published, it became an instant success and emerged as a popular souvenir for domestic and foreign visitors to Zhuxianzhen.

"Now the woodprint New Year pictures are playing the role of a 'calling card' that introduces Zhuxianzhen to the rest of the world", commented Yao Jingtang.

Zhang Tingxu sculpting a wooden board.

Zhang used a paper cutter left over by family ancestors to cut a bundle of paper. The knife is already 100-year old and could cut 500 pieces of paper a time, says Zhang.

The first volume of the New Year pictures album, jointly published by Yao Jingtang and Zhang Tingxu, was quite popular with experts, scholars and collectors.

Zhang's family workshop of New Year pictures printing.

⬆ All woodprint New Year pictures are made manually.
⬆ Age-old New Year pictures collected at Zhang's home, all left over by his ancestors.
⬇ Senior citizens in Zhuxianzhen often recall the prosperity of the town in old times.

The fun-seeker

Photos by Chen Gengsheng

In the eyes of his friends, Min Jiali is an expert in looking for fun and enjoying the thrill of life. While hobbies like photography, aeromodelling, cross-country driving, air gliding, and amateur radio operation are still fresh and unfamiliar terms to most people, Min has made them an integral part of his everyday life.

A native of Zhengzhou City, capital of central China's Henan Province, Min started his business career in the early 1980s. He worked successively as a designer, advertising agent, florist, house decorator and stationery salesman before opening a mechanical parts processing factory of his own. After saving a considerable amount of money in the banks, Min suddenly decided to quit business and spend most of the time enjoying the real fun of life.

In 1990, Min became a photography enthusiast and spent 200, 000 yuan (24,100 dollars) on cameras, zoom lenses and other state-of-the-art photographic devices. To take pictures, he traveled a lot and left footprints in Hainan, the southernmost island province of China, the no man's land in Tibet and even in the vast Taklimakan desert. While he took interest in aeromodelling, he spent several thousand yuan (hundreds of dollars) purchasing parts of plane models, and then co-worked with his son to assemble them piece by piece. For some period, he was addicted to flying, with a paraglider on his back and feeling as free as a bird.

When he started to be enchanted with cross-country driving, he drove along the Yellow River and reached the desolate western hinterland of the country. In April, 2002, he initiated a program called "touring the roof of the world", in which he and 30 friends drove 12 jeeps all the way to Tibet along the landslide-prone Sichuan-Tibet highway.

At home in Zhengzhou, Min is an expert-level HAM, or amateur radio operator. He can talk to HAMs worldwide from his home, which has been turned into a radio communication center in the past years. He enjoys the fun of making friends with unknown people, learning their languages and understanding their cultures.

Though Min has broad interests and many ways to seek fun, he claims that he has done everything out of his strong curiosity, or a desire to learn more about the colorful world and life.

Min and his friends often drive out to enjoy the beauty of nature.
Flying plane models outdoors is great fun.
The outdoor antenna for radio communications, which Min has made himself, is close to professional standards.

⋒ Assembling plane models along with his son.
⋒ Serving customers in his photo shop.
⋐ A wireless radio transceiver on the jeep enables Min to communicate with others at any time.

A female boss on the Balkor Street

Photos by Jiao Bo

In 7th Century A.D., Songzan-gambo, founder of the ancient Tibet kingdom, ordered the construction of the beautiful Jokhang temple, which attracted numerous pilgrims. For one year after another, under the tireless feet of pilgrims who piously toured around the Jokhang temple again and again, the Balkor Street had come into existence. The street became the original center of today's Lhasa City, which covers an area of 523 square kilometers.

The 1-km-long Balkor Street used to be a simple earth road, but now has been paved with stone slabs. For over 1,000 years, from dawn to dusk, this street has always been crowded with countless scripture rotators. A traditional ritual in Tibetan Buddhism, scripture-rotation refers to Buddhist believers continuously circling around the Jokhang temple from left to right, with each round symbolizing the recital of one Buddhist scripture. Medog Zhoigar, 69, is a successful businesswoman on the Balkor Street, and every morning she would first take her scripture-rotation along the an-cient lane before starting any business activities.

As an old resident in Lhasa, Medog Zhoigar had experienced both poverty and affluence in her life. Before the democratic reforms in Tibet, which ended the century-old feudal serfdom, Medog Zhoigar and her family had led an extremely difficult life. After the 1959 reforms, the lives of most Tibetans have gradually turned for the better, but the Medog Zhoigar family still often encountered financial difficulties. When her grandson was to enter the school, she had to borrow his five-yuan (60 cents) tuition fees from the neighbors. In 1980, when China just launched its reform and opening-up drive, Medog Zhoigar sold her family furniture for capital and started her own business. By running a vendor's stall on the Balkor Street, Medog Zhoigar gradually shook off poverty and started to lead a well-off life. In 1996, she invested 700,000 yuan (84,333 dollars) to purchase nearly 200 square meters of roadside houses on the Balkor Street and then rented them out to other businesspeople at more than 20,000 yuan (2,400 dollars) a month. Her grandson, Cering Wanggyai, and his wife also rented one of these houses to sell traditional Tibetan costumes. The young couple could earn 70,000 to 80,000 yuan (8433 to 9638 dollars) each year, but every month they still have to pay 1,000 yuan (120 dollars) of house rent to their grandmother. "This is what we call 'family contracting'," said Cering Wanggyai.

The family of Medog Zhoigar also lived on the Balkor Street. Looking out from the balcony of her three-story house, the golden roof of the Jokhang temple seems to be just a few feet away. The husband of Medog Zhoigar has already retired, but he cares little about the family business. Instead he often goes to metropolises like Beijing, Tianjin and Shanghai for sightseeing, or, in the joking words of other family members, for "market investigation". However, Medog Zhoigar has been used to hard work and every day she helps her granddaughter-in-law to attend to business. When she returns home in the evening, Medog Zhoigar often sings some traditional Tibetan opera for fun, while her husband will dance to the strains of her singing and her children and grandchildren will applaud and acclaim.

⬆ Though nearly in her 70s, Medog Zhoigar still pays much attention to her appearance.
⬇ Every morning, Medog Zhoigar and her husband will take a scripture-rotation on the Balkor Street.

① The female boss asks every customer to leave
  comments and suggestions on the service.
② Medog Zhoigar was very pleased to see the
  changes on the Balkor Street over these years.

144

⬆ Medog Zhoigar and her family like to decorate the balcony of their house with fresh flowers.

⬇ A traditional Tibetan dance excites everyone in the house.

The urbanite-turned-farmer

Photos by Jiang Hao

Autumn arrived and Wang Fengyun savored the sweet joy of harvest seeing fruits hanging all over the 200-strong plum trees and over-600 peach trees in her garden.

Wang used to be a saleswoman in a store in Licheng District of Jinan City, capital of east China's Shandong Province. As her store suffered losses and started to sack employees several years ago, Wang lost her first job. With no complaints, Wang acquired a driver license and found a new job as a taxi driver. However, three years later, the government decided to remove all minivan taxis from the city streets, and Wang, unable to afford a new car, lost her job

again.

However, while working as a taxi driver, Wang had learned a lot through listening to radio programs and reading newspapers. She knew that the government was encouraging the development of a "green agriculture", or an environment-friendly and pollution-free agriculture with high efficiency, in the rural areas. She also knew that many farmers had already become well-off thanks to the application of new agricultural technologies. "Why can't I start a new career in the countryside?!" she asked herself. So after some discussion with her husband, Wang made up her mind to go to the countryside to seek success.

Wang believed that the most lucrative farming sector was fruits growing and that high economic returns could be achieved only through growing well-known, high-quality fruit varieties. At the end of 2000, she invested 40,000 yuan (4,800 dollars) to lease two mu (1,300 square meters) of land in a village not far from her home and build two high-standard greenhouses. She also purchased some new varieties of fruit trees. As the fruit trees needed daily care, Wang moved into the village where her greenhouses were built and started to lead a farmer's life.

With no farming experiences, Wang had encountered many a difficulty in learning fruit growing. She bought many books on agricultural technologies and also modestly sought assistance from other fruit growers in the village. Gradually, she grasped the basic skills for fruit tree planting and caring. However, some of the field labor, such as transporting tree saplings or shielding the greenhouse with a nearly-50-kg thatch mattress every day, was so tough that even a male adult would find it too hard to bear. Other work like pruning the trees, watering and fertilizing the land was also no easy as both physical strength and technical skills were needed. To the surprise of many, Wang had endured all these hardships and accomplished everything all alone. However, in summer her clothes were often soaked with sweat and her skin was seriously suntanned, while in winter her hands chapped in the cold winds and often developed frostbites.

Since the greenhouses were built, Wang has seldom returned home and had to leave her son to the care of his grandparents. In autumn, she invited the whole family to her garden and let them share the joy of harvest. With her wisdom and sweat, Wang has proved her belief: as long as you work hard and try your best, you will always be the master of your own destiny.

⬆ Though once a car driver, Wang found it difficult to ride a tricycle.
⬆ Unable to return home often, Wang missed her son very much.
◐ Wang was overjoyed to see the fruit harvest.

In her spare time, Wang visited stores to buy some pretty clothes for herself. She never forgot to make herself look decent after a day of field labor.

Wang consulted an agricultural expert while purchasing fruit seeds.

Time to relax: take a cup of tea and watch some TV.

After years of harsh labor, Wang saw a changed self in the mirror.

To keep it warm inside, Wang had to cover the greenhouse with a nearly-50-kg thatch mattress every day.

The Olympic fever in the Beijing Hutongs

Photos by Liu Yingyi

Every morning before 6 a.m., Master Li, a Beijing resident in his 60s, has got up and started practicing Taijiquan, or shadow boxing, in the Hutong (alley) where he lives. Li, who started to learn Kung Fu, or traditional Chinese martial arts, as a teenager, has kept on practicing for decades. Moreover, he is also a member of the Beijing Homing Pigeons Association, as one of the homing pigeons trained by him has traveled to east China's Fujian Province, several thousand kilometers away from Beijing.

In the ancient and tranquil Beijing Hutongs, or narrow alleys with traditional residential compounds lining up on both sides, there are many sports lovers and daily exercisers like Master Li. When dawns break or dusks fall, almost every piece of the open space in the Hutongs is occupied by people doing exercises or engaging in sports activities. Under the trees there are senior citizens playing Chinese chess. The girls like to skip and dance over chains of rubber bands, while the boys prefer football or basketball. Though there is no standard football pitch and the baskets have to be fixed on wire poles or compound walls, the Hutong residents could still have great fun.

In recent years, the municipal government of Beijing has installed many modern body-building or exercising devices, such as parallel bars, seesaws and table tennis facilities, in the Hutongs and residents' communities. This has prompted more local residents to form the habit of exercising. Beijing's successful bid to host the 2008 Summer Olympics has further fueled this sports fever in this ancient capital. Some traditional sports events long forgotten or ignored, such as shuttlecock kicking, kite flying and homing pigeon training, have revived, while new sports forms like slide board, roller skating and badminton are also thriving. All these have added much vitality to the ancient Hutongs.

In the Qianmen Primary School located in the Tongle Hutong, whose students are exclusively kids from the nearby Hutongs, there is an amateur roller skating team. Consisting of students only, the team had been invited to perform at the opening ceremony of the 10th National University Games. Every day after school, on their way home, students in the team would put on their roller skates and practice in the Hutongs. Their superb skills often attract residents or passers-by in the Hutongs to become their spectators. A sports teacher of the school said: "Our school will always keep this roller skating team. When Beijing plays host to the Olympic Games in 2008, I will lead my students to perform at the opening ceremony."

Kids in the Hutongs playing a "unique" table tennis game.
The narrow yet long Hutongs are ideal lanes for roller skaters.

CHINESE STORIES

152

153

Every day Hutong residents take group exercises by following radio instructions.
Old neighbors are often "lifetime opponents" on chess board.
In the narrow alleys, it's common for the shuttlecock to go to rooftop.

① With a bicycle basket tied to the street lamp, basketball lovers in the Hutongs enjoy no less fun than NBA fans.
② "Amateur gymnasts" exercising on the newly-installed parallel bars.
⊃ An intense football match in an ancient alley.

The Oriental Dancing Goddess

○ Photos by Wang Yao

Chen Ailian, a famous Chinese dancer, has just celebrated the 50th anniversary of the debut of her dancing career. In 1952, when she was picked from an orphanage in Shanghai, China's largest city, to become a member of the dance troupe affiliated to the Central Drama Institute in Beijing, Chen didn't believe that dancing would be her lifetime career. "At that time I thought dancing was a very shallow form of art," she recalled. However, her view started to change after watching a documentary titled "The ballet masters of the Soviet Union", which introduced four ballet classics produced in the former Soviet Union. "I was overwhelmed by the beauty of ballet, and came to realize that one could take great pleasure in enjoying a dancing performance," said Chen.

In 1954, Chen became a student of the Beijing Dance School. In 1959, she graduated with an excellent study record and became a faculty member of the school. In the same year, she was selected to be the chief dancer in two ballet classics staged in China for first time, namely the Swan Lake and the Mermaid, and became famous overnight. In 1962, Chen participated in the 8th World Youth Get-Together Festival hosted by Finland as a representative of the Chinese dancers. With her superb presentation of dances like "A night of flowers and moon on the spring river", the "snake dance", the "bow dance" and the "straw-hat dance", Chen won several gold medals at the festival and also earned the fame as an "Oriental Dancing Goddess", as the local media had put it.

In 1963, Chen joined the China Opera and Ballet Theater and served as a leading dancer in the theater. She played the leading role in several operas and ballets and gradually established herself as China's No.1 ballet dancer. In 1980, Chen became the first Chinese ballet dancer to give a personal dance show. At that show she presented Chinese classic dances, ballet dances, Chinese and foreign folk dances, as well as modern dances. She also played 10 different female roles, both ancient and modern, Chinese and foreign. In 1987, Chen staged another personal dance show, at which she made a successful attempt to combine Chinese traditional dances with modern dances.

Though she is already more than 60 years old now, Chen has no intention to quit the stage. She keeps on practicing every day, with no breaks even on holidays. She believes that a dancer will not turn mature until he or she is 30 years old. "Before the age of 20, all one can do is just build muscles and learn basic skills. Only after 30 could one acquire a comprehensive and profound understanding of the art of dance," she says. She says it's a pity that most Chinese dancers have chosen to quit stage when they are still young, causing a waste of talents and a stagnation in the development of Chinese dancing.

At the end of 2002, Chen returned to her birthplace Shanghai to hold an exhibition on her 50-year dancing career, as well as stage a personal dance show. "I hope other mature dancers will gain confidence from my example and stay longer on the stage," she said sincerely.

⊙ No pains, no gains.

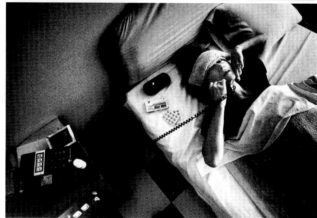

⦿ Though in her 60s, Chen keeps on practicing every day.

⦿ Chen won't stop her work even when falling ill.

⦿ For her students, Chen is a very strict teacher.

⬆ A dancing star herself, Chen has also trained many good dancers.
➥ A moment of peace after an exhausting performance.

图书在版编目(CIP)数据

中国百姓故事. 2/ 焦波编.
－北京：五洲传播出版社，2003.12
ISBN 7-5085-0386-4

I.中…

II.焦…

III.社会生活－中国－画册－英文

IV.D669-64

中国版本图书馆 CIP 数据核字(2003)第 120707 号

序　　言：梁晓声
撰　　文：苏晓环
责任编辑：焦　波
图片编辑：胡艳丽
翻　　译：周效政
校　　对：张行军
装帧设计：田　林　傅晓斌
制　　作：北京原色印象文化艺术中心

中国百姓故事(二)

出版发行：五洲传播出版社
通讯地址：中国北京北三环中路 31 号
邮政编码：100088
电　　话：8610-82008174 83793335
网　　址：www.cicc.org.cn
印　　刷：北京华联印刷有限公司
开　　本：1/16　889×1194
印　　张：10.5
版　　次：2003 年 12 月第一版 2003 年 12 月第一次印刷
书　　号：ISBN 7-5085-0386-4/D · 170
定　　价：150 元